Dale

For your amusement

Dick

Great Good Fortune

Carl A. Vigeland

HOUGHTON MIFFLIN COMPANY

BOSTON

1986

GREAT
GOOD
FORTUNE

HOW
HARVARD
MAKES
ITS
MONEY

A RICHARD TODD BOOK

Library of Congress Cataloging-in-Publication Data

Vigeland, Carl A.
Great good fortune.

1. Harvard University — Finance. 2. Harvard
University — Public relations. 3. Endowments —
Massachusetts — Cambridge. 4. Educational fund
raising — Massachusetts — Cambridge. I. Title.
LD2115.V55 1986   378.744'4   86-4711
ISBN 0-395-36231-8

Printed in the United States of America

P 10 9 8 7 6 5 4 3 2 1

Lines from "Tercentenary Trinity" by David McCord are
reprinted by permission of *The Harvard Lampoon*.

for Bonnie

A Business to Run

TO SPEND ANY TIME at Harvard is to be impressed especially by two things: the vitality of the institution and the reticence of the men — for they are nearly all men — who run it. This duality, which manifests itself in a variety of ways, makes learning how Harvard works a challenge. Harvard invites attention; most Harvard men spurn it. Harvard's public self is extraordinarily rich and arresting; its private core is unusually hidden and elusive.

The reasons for this reticence speak to something very basic in the institution. Harvard ought not to have anything to hide, but it does have much to lose. The stakes for which it plays are enormous: a $3 billion endowment, a $650 million annual budget, a worldwide reputation. Money makes that preeminence possible.

There is a mystique to Harvard; money makes the mystique, money to do the things Harvard says it can do and then does. But having money is more than a way for Harvard to pay bills. Harvard is bigger than any one person and money helps define that. Money sets limits. Raising it also puts people through hoops, involving them in activities that are far from Harvard's ideals as a university.

Harvard always needs money, and getting it requires Harvard to solicit its alumni, manage its endowment, and tap other sources. Harvard's dynamic money making links its relationship with alumni to the management of its endowment, its decisions on major capital expenditures to its policies on major issues. But Harvard, a private, nonprofit institution, is the leader in an un-regulated industry, and it is accountable to no stockholders. To boast about how it conducts its affairs is inimical to the competitive advantage it enjoys.

After I started work on this book, one Harvard official wrote me saying he didn't think it would be good for philanthropy. Another refused to speak with me until he'd discussed my request with the president of the university's Board of Overseers. These encounters, and others like them, were instructive; so were the exceptions. When I told some of his old colleagues I planned to interview former Harvard president Pusey, they said he was a bitter man. I shouldn't call him, they advised. I wrote him anyway, and he responded that he would be happy to see me.

Nathan Marsh Pusey represents a part of Harvard's past that does not square with its present. Late in his administration, he was responsible for bringing in police to remove students occupying Harvard's University Hall in a 1969 protest over the Vietnam War. That single divisive event overshadowed the achievements of his presidency, and when he retired two years later there were many who were glad to see him go.

We met in the lobby of the Harvard Club in New York. Behind us, through a glass door, a few people in one of the club's dining rooms were finishing a late lunch. Others passed by, on their way to the barbershop or shoeshine stand in the basement or the squash courts upstairs. No one stopped to say hello to Pusey, though few could not have known who he was or failed to have been taken by how well he looked at seventy-seven, with that same extraordinarily clear complexion and white hair. How exactly proper and contented he seemed.

Pusey touched the collar pin on his shirt and patted the front of his suitcoat to be certain the middle button was fastened. We walked together through the dining room into Harvard Hall, a room three stories high, its walls paneled, oriental rugs on the floor, and a Christmas tree standing in front of the huge windows that face onto West 45th Street. We saw an old alumnus who was sleeping in one of the leather chairs, and Pusey smiled. We took seats across from each other at a small reading table, with a brass lamp on the wall next to it. Sitting erect, Pusey took out his glasses and, after adjusting their placement, rested his hands on the table and began speaking in a calm, slightly musical voice.

"When I left Harvard, it had nothing to do with the student disturbances. It was clear that Harvard was going into a new period, and I felt I had done all I could do at Harvard."

By and large, Pusey's memory was still sharp; he'd forget the name of a former dean occasionally — in fact there was one dean he could not even remember appointing — but he had a vivid picture of Harvard in his head. At first, after he had moved to New York, alumni had come up to him to say how sorry they were for the bad time he had had, and he thought, "It hadn't occurred to me it was bad. Being president of Harvard was a great joy."

His presidency was distinguished by staunch support of free speech during the McCarthy era — with four other Harvard officials, Pusey earned a commendation from the American Civil Liberties Union — and a talent for fund raising, which culminated in the $82.5 million Program for Harvard College. Completed in 1960, that campaign was at the time the largest ever undertaken in private higher education in the United States. He had consciously stayed out of Harvard affairs since Derek Bok — the man he had chosen as dean of Harvard Law School — became president. But Pusey served on the executive committee of the recent $350 million Harvard Campaign.

"I was worried that Harvard would rely on its past, great donors, and I argued with Derek and others about this. I felt the campaign had to find Harvard donors who were younger. I guess it did."

Certain that what he called "the troubles" had started elsewhere, Pusey said he had believed Harvard students "were smart enough not to get involved." He was talking about the protests in the late 1960s, when he could remember a well-known student radical from California coming to Cambridge, "his way paid by a television company, and I remember seeing him pass by Straus Hall. There were lots of cameras there, but no other people."

Citing as an example the occupation of the Columbia University library, Pusey continued: "By the time of the University Hall incident, I had persuaded myself and the Corporation that we were not going to accept this. There was going to be a bang, but it was going to be over in two weeks. If not, people would have come in from elsewhere. I can't prove calling in the police was the wisest course, but I'd do it again.

"Some people afterwards thought of me as a horrible character. My own personal disappointment was not with the students. There were never more than a few who wanted to be revolutionaries. The great majority did not, but they were unhappy with the Vietnam War. There were a lot of nice, innocent kids who were manipulated by some crafty characters.

"My disappointment was with certain members of the faculty who failed to give the guidance they could have. Some of them lost their nerve.

"I've never said this to anyone but my wife — but deep in my heart there was a disenchantment in me with the Harvard faculty, and I had to go out and make speeches about the wonderful scholars they were. I couldn't go out and say that anymore.

"Bitterness? No. I was sad. What happened was beneath Harvard's dignity. I loved Harvard. There are still one or two faculty members, if I see them, there is no joy. I suppose they feel the same way about me."

The club was quiet, save for the rustling of newspaper pages being turned by someone on the other side of Harvard Hall and a faint rumble through the exterior brick walls of traffic passing by outside. The city seemed far away, though Times Square was just a five-minute walk from the clubhouse. Pusey never hurried as he spoke. At times he seemed almost lost in a trance.

"Derek was a youngster when he was selected. I had my eye on him, but I stayed out of the search. I was very happy when he was chosen. The one thing I felt badly about was that he said before he accepted that Sissela wasn't going to be 'a president's wife.' My wife, Anne, was extraordinarily gifted at getting along with faculty wives and others. That's important in an academic community — if Harvard isn't too big now to be called a community." Intended solely as an affectionate tribute to Mrs. Pusey, the remark was uttered without rancor, nor with reference to Sissela Bok's career as a scholar and professor — which made her husband a faculty spouse.

The man in the leather chair was still sleeping as we passed him, left Harvard Hall, and stopped at the coat check. Very deliberately, Pusey put first one arm then the other into the sleeves of his overcoat, buttoned it, and placed his hat on his head. Passing by the cigar stand and through the lobby, Pusey walked out of the door and into the city, where the afternoon light was rapidly fading to dusk.

I met many other Harvard men as I conducted my research for this book. None were as serene, as seductively radiant, as Nathan Pusey. Some were blunt, while others practiced more subtle verbal deception, trying to kill my questions with kindness. Yet at the same time I sensed in certain people a desire to talk, an underlying wish to be rid of the spell of silence Harvard casts on its chosen.

"Before Bok," one such Harvard official told me, "Harvard wasn't a business. It was a confederation. It had plentiful resources. Academic successes. Alumni gave their time and money. Then, gradually, or at some point in time, post-Pusey, Harvard had to face that it, too, had to manage its affairs better. It began to recognize, 'We've got a business to run.' It began to professionalize the process of running a large institution. The golden age of academia was coming into the real world." Harvard could no longer get by just because it was Harvard.

"If there were a criticism of my administration," Nathan Pusey said, with a measure of pride rather than regret, "it would be that I was trying still to run Harvard as though it were small." Derek Bok has no such luxury. His Harvard has grown tremendously, and the illusion of innocence Pusey evokes has gone irrevocably. "We're doing hard jobs here," Bok once told me, "working as hard as we can." Coming from a man whose reticence is legend, that admission was tantamount to a revelation, a small human crack in an immense institutional wall.

Mr. Bok's Empire

FROM A HILL on the state highway that enters Cambridge from the west, Harvard University seems all spires and steeples, set within an urban expanse. Boston borders Cambridge, with the Charles River running between the two cities. From the Boston side of the Charles, Harvard appears suddenly around a big bend in the river. Looming over a solitary scull skimming the water's surface, Harvard is a haven in the midst of signs for the Massachusetts Turnpike, new hotels, and busy streets. Built in the 1930s, Harvard's neo-Georgian river Houses, or dormitories, anchor the campus, which winds back into Cambridge to Harvard Square and Harvard Yard in a changing series of architectural styles. Among the university's newest buildings, a five-foot-square guardhouse by a gate to Harvard Yard cost $57,000, including architect's fees and landscaping. A few of Harvard's major buildings are modern, but ivy on old brick still predominates. Not long ago, Harvard said it was going to remove the ivy because of the damage the vines wreaked on weak mortises, but student and alumni protest forced a reversal of the decision.

Students from around the world compete to attend Harvard. "For generation after generation," wrote Henry Adams in his *Education,* "Adamses and Brookses and Boylstons and Gorhams had gone to Harvard College, and although none of them, as far as known, had ever done any good there, or thought himself the better for it, custom, social ties, convenience, and, above all, economy, kept each generation in the track. Any other education," he continued, "would have required a serious effort, but no one took Harvard College seriously. All went there because their friends went there, and the College was their ideal of social self-respect."

Among the approximately thirteen thousand applicants to a Harvard/Radcliffe class today, there are still a few for whom the college is simply "their ideal of social self-respect." And Harvard admits some of them. But since the end of World War II, the demographics represented by the Harvard student body have been changing. A Harvard class now includes more graduates of public high schools than private prep schools. Since the 1960s, Harvard has built and refined recruitment programs to attract minority students, with mixed success — 181 blacks were admitted to the Harvard Class of 1988, but only 106 accepted Harvard's offer. And since 1975 at Harvard, quotas for the number of men and women, who used to be admitted separately — the men to Harvard and women to Radcliffe — have been abolished. Today, a single, joint, highly selective admissions process chooses students without regard to sex. More men than women apply, however, and this apparently accounts for the disparity in male versus female acceptances and matriculations: 938 men and 699 women comprise the Class of 1988. The highest percentage of students come from the Northeastern United States, continuing Harvard's long identification with its location.

"Boston First Family statistics do not alone tell the story of Harvard and its interrelationship with the Proper Bostonian," Cleveland Amory wrote in 1947. "Sixty-one members of the Proper Bostonian's two ranking families, the Cabots and Lowells, have beaten a path to Harvard's doors in the past hundred

years, but even this figure falls short in explaining the extent of
his connection with the place. Harvard is actually a major port
of the Proper Bostonian's total existence, of his adult life in some
respects even more than his college life. . . .

"Socially speaking, Harvard and Boston could hardly be anything but inseparable. . . . Edmund Quincy laid down First
Family law memorably on this point . . . 'If a man's in there,' he
used to say, tapping his Harvard Triennial Catalog, containing a
complete list of Harvard graduates, 'that's who he is. If he isn't,
who is he?' " Looking at an updated list, Mr. Quincy would see
many names he didn't recognize.

By 1985–86, proper Bostonians and upstarts from elsewhere
were paying more than $15,000 for undergraduate tuition,
room, and board. To the parents of some of these students, this
sum represented no sacrifice, while to others it meant the misery
of filing detailed financial aid applications and scrimping on
other parts of the family's budget. No single facet of Harvard's
budget was, therefore, pricklier, yet it was accepted by most people with resignation. Harvard cited many of the same reasons it
does for its fund raising as the causes for another hefty tuition
increase — boosting faculty salaries and paying for physical plant
renovations chief among them. In setting the exact tuition
charge, Harvard officials waited until they knew as much as possible about costs for the following year; but they also surveyed
the competition. Yale and Princeton, for example, had both announced tuition levels over $15,000. The Harvard figure was
more than double what it was a decade before.

Like its competitors, Harvard always points out that tuition
pays only a portion of the cost of educating its students — in
Harvard's case, about one-third. But this estimate begs a question Harvard and rival schools avoid discussing. How, with student bodies of differing sizes, faculty salaries of varying scales,
endowments of unequal earnings, and physical plants of little
comparability — how can the figures for tuition at different
schools be so similar?

The rough answer at Harvard is that not all costs are fixed, and some are set relative to what Harvard thinks certain revenues will be. Revenue from students — the largest single category in Harvard's income, or about $193 million in 1983–84 — is not simply a factor of costs but of what Harvard believes the market will bear. But the real answer to the question of oligopolistic pricing among prestigious schools is much more complicated, and it includes a fact of academic finance that has vexed administrators from the beginning. What are the costs? Just such items as faculty salaries and heating fuel, or the overhead at the library, too? Should they be borne equally by, say, the student who plays intercollegiate ice hockey and another who sleeps through breakfast? And however a tuition figure is computed, what is its limit? At what point, despite its policy of "aid-blind" admissions (which few other schools can afford to maintain), does Harvard begin losing students because the cost of four years at Harvard is now almost that of the median price of a home? And, conversely, why not charge three times the amount, if that is closer to the "cost," since the parents of many Harvard students can pay that, and put everyone who can't on scholarship? Or, estimating the extrinsic value of a Harvard education by occupation, should tuition be set *after* a student's graduation, at one level for those who join the Peace Corps and another for investment bankers?

Questions about tuition and an array of other academic problems, including curriculum considerations, tenure decisions, and resource allocation, underlie Harvard's budgetary concerns. While there is little time for personal or institutional reflection, the president and his five vice presidents in Massachusetts Hall, which has become a kind of Oval Office of higher education, go about their work with an air of high purpose. "A lot of the issues," says Daniel Steiner, vice president and general counsel, "are serious policy questions with difficult moral and ethical overtones." A lot of the issues are also riskier, requiring Harvard to exploit opportunities it used to ignore. Harvard is playing a faster, more sophisticated and complicated game, and it is no longer declared the winner before the contest begins.

In the mid-1980s, while the collective anxiety of the United States was focused on nuclear weapons, international terrorism, and a cure for AIDS, the nation's oldest and wealthiest institution of higher education was moving simultaneously on more financial fronts than any one person could direct. Even Derek Bok, with his purported "empirical grasp of detail," had to be selective, nor were money matters the only subject before him. It is in the nature of a university, especially one of Harvard's size and stature, that new problems — or old ones in different dress — constantly present themselves.

Only a generation before, Nathan Pusey described Harvard as "a kind of island of light in a very widespread darkness." No such simple metaphor now serves Harvard, where the annual debt service of nearly $50 million exceeds the entire annual budget of many fine small colleges. Harvard has produced more United States presidents, Supreme Court justices, and members of Congress than any other institution; numbers among its graduates Henry David Thoreau, John Updike, 226 Rhodes scholars, and more top corporate executives than the second-place school by a factor of two to one; and counts the Nobel laureates and Pulitzer Prize winners on its faculty by the dozen. But the education of its students and the research of professors are dependent on money. As Derek Bok's Harvard prepared to celebrate "350 years of higher education in America," it had become an institution whose reliance on alumni giving, need for endowment income and growth, and dependence on federal dollars are not incidental but fundamental.

When Ronald Reagan's secretary for education, William J. Bennett, suggested that universities receiving federal funds be rated, "so the higher education consumer can be confident he is purchasing a sound product," Derek Bok reacted with unsurprising skepticism. Serious and high-minded, Bok invariably sounded at such times as though he were speaking for Western civilization. The two men, who had publicly clashed before over such issues as the Reagan administration's proposed cuts in student aid, couldn't have been further apart.

"The Department of Education has an obligation to the students it assists with financial aid and to the taxpayers whose funds it disburses," Bennett told the American Council on Education's 1985 convention in Miami. Responding in Cambridge to a reporter's questions about the speech, Derek Bok said he "didn't know of any adequate measures to do the task" of rating. Bok, who had once called Bennett "a novice who may improve with time," sounded personally affronted over the galling prospect of an inferior's presumption. No different from the tenor of Harvard's response to critics of its investment policies or its construction projects, Bok's tone was that of a plant owner challenged by a union chief who wants to see the company's books.

Derek Bok's job puts extraordinary constraints on what he can do each day at the same time that it permits him to do almost anything he wants. He is the man at the top, but frequently he ends up in the middle. Because he is president of Harvard, there are constant demands on his time; yet for the same reason, because he is president, he can initiate activities that others can't. Because he is president, he is obliged to attend many meetings and functions; but he can write to almost any civic, corporate, or educational leaders in the country and they'll gladly agree to see him. Someone else has to take many of his phone calls, but he can call anyone he wants — a movie star, a senator, the president of the United States — and the call will be put through. Many educators hang on his every word. He has to watch what he says to the press and deny many of the requests for interviews, but if he feels like writing a letter to *The New York Times* it will be printed. When the Reverend Jesse Jackson spoke at a Harvard rally in April 1985, Bok had to leave his own office, for fear of becoming barricaded inside it by Harvard students protesting Harvard's investments in companies that do business in South Africa. Yet Bok could — and would, later in the spring, on another campus — meet with Jackson personally, not because he is Derek Bok but because he is Harvard's president. He lives a life of great restraint and great freedom. It is a life in the goldfish bowl, but he is the fisherman as well as the fish.

Money — its quest, its management, and, to a lesser extent, its expenditure — sharpens this conflict. It provides an edge in Bok's professional life. Harvard seemingly has enough money, enough power, to do whatever it pleases. But the pressures on its finances have increased tremendously, and because Harvard *is* Harvard, what it does with its money has an impact that reaches far beyond Harvard Yard. Derek Bok's understanding of this heightens the inner clash between what he wants to do and can, what he has to do and can't. Almost anything he says or writes is related to money. Almost any decision he makes has a financial ramification, and he makes almost no important decisions that aren't criticized by someone.

A portrait of Harvard's president in his own words — in print or in person — would win no awards for confession. Bok dismisses the interest of others in his work as though there were something inherently distasteful in talking about oneself. With a carefully timed pause for laughter, he sums up his time allocation by recalling the remark of a Stanford president who said he had no idea how he planned his day; nothing a president did mattered. Bok admits to "occasionally" looking at his calendar, to see what he can squeeze in. Other people make his schedule for him. He won't say he's a lucky man, but he admits he's not unlucky. "I've never been sick," he boasts. Protective of his privacy and Harvard's, he has been criticized for a lack of charisma, of soul. But critics who quarrel with him over not only the style but the substance of many of his decisions agree with Derek Bok that there is much to protect at Harvard.

The most recent in a very long line of Harvard presidents, Bok sometimes speaks of himself in the third person, as if to emphasize the pride of his office. He and the other six members of the Harvard Corporation are the oldest self-perpetuating corporation in the Western Hemisphere. The charter granted in 1650 by the

General Court of the Massachusetts Bay Colony to the President and Fellows of Harvard College, as the Corporation still is formally called, bestows an antiquity on Harvard, giving a historic dimension to the Corporation's actions no other American group can claim. Even the evocative language of the charter puts a patina on the body:

> Whereas through the good hand of God many well devoted persons have beene and dayly are mooved and stirred up to give and bestowe sundry guiftes legacies landes and Revennewes for the advancement of all good literature artes and Sciences in Harvard Colledge in Cambridge in the County of Middlesex and to the maintenance of the Praesident and Fellowes and for all accomodacons of Buildinges and all other necessary provisions that may conduce to the education of the English and Indian youth of this Country in knowledge: and godliness. It is therefore ordered and enacted by this Court and the Aucthority thereof That for the furthering of so good a worke and for the purposes aforesaid from henceforth that the said Colledge in Cambridge in Middlesex in New England shalbe a Corporation Consisting of seaven persons (to wit) a President Five Fellowes and a Treasurer or Bursar.

More than three hundred years later, Derek Bok wrote in his 1982 book, *Beyond the Ivory Tower:* "After World War II . . . the image of the ivory tower grew obsolete. Instead, a vast and intricate network of relationships arose linking universities to other major institutions in the society." The book, subtitled "Social Responsibilities of the Modern University" and clearly intended for a wide audience, addresses grand themes illustrated with Bok's analysis of his Harvard experience. But it never clearly states that within Harvard itself there is now a kind of "vast and intricate network," linking fund raising and alumni relations, endowment management and South Africa, Harvard's money and Harvard's power. Nathan Pusey's small community has become Derek Bok's big business, and the motive for the change has been money — how it is raised, how it is managed, and how it is used.

Bok, who takes an inordinate interest in the university's grounds, often stooping to pick up litter in his path, might have made a good landscape architect. Instead, he has spent almost his entire life as an academic and administrator at Harvard. Photographs of Bok when he became president in 1971 show a smiling young man, his hair black, the circles under his eyes barely visible. The eyes, always penetrating, have become more wary over the years, and much of his hair has turned gray. In his mid-fifties, Derek Bok is still young by some standards. But he's had this job longer than most college and university presidents stay on in their posts. The pressures are real, but Bok has tried to keep them impersonal. Ill at ease before large groups or in impromptu exchanges, he retreats to the realms of procedure and policy when he has a choice, avoiding both formal confrontation and casual give-and-take.

Born in 1930 in Bryn Mawr, Pennsylvania, Bok is the son of a prominent judge. His grandfather Edward Bok emigrated to the United States from Holland, married into the Curtis family, which owned the Curtis Publishing Company, and became the editor of *Ladies' Home Journal*. Edward Bok's 1920 autobiography won a Pulitzer Prize. His grandson graduated from Stanford University in 1951, where he was a Renaissance man — bright, handsome, wealthy, charming, and a good basketball and clarinet player. After finishing Harvard Law School in 1954, Derek Bok spent a year in Paris as a Fulbright scholar, then went to Washington, where he got a master's degree in economics from George Washington University and did his military service in the judge advocate's office.

In 1958, at the age of twenty-eight, Bok returned to Harvard as an assistant professor at the Law School; just three years later came appointment as a full professor, and seven years after that, at the age of thirty-eight, dean of the Law School. An expert on labor law, he edited a 1962 casebook on that subject with Harvard Law professor Archibald Cox, the man Richard Nixon would later fire as Watergate prosecutor, and co-authored a 1970 volume, *Labor and the American Community,* with John T. Dunlop, also a Harvard professor and a final candidate to succeed

Nathan Pusey. In 1955 Bok married Sissela Ann Myrdal, both of whose parents were Nobel Prize winners. The author of two landmark books in ethics, she now teaches at Brandeis University.

Two months shy of his forty-first birthday, Derek Bok was selected as the twenty-fifth president of Harvard, the first non-alumnus of Harvard College to hold that position in three centuries. He inherited from his predecessor an administrative machinery that was woefully understaffed. Pusey, who saw himself as the person who "directs the correspondence of the university," had only one vice president. His development, or fund-raising, office operated as it had for a generation, with little reliance on modern marketing techniques or cognizance of Harvard's changing alumni demographics. Harvard's endowment management under Pusey was so old-fashioned that a regular feature was an oral report by the treasurer to the other members of the Harvard Corporation on what Harvard had bought and sold since they'd last met.

Bok's first priority was to put the house in order, and he moved quickly to do so. Within five years, Harvard had formed a separate company to manage its investment portfolio (the Harvard Management Company), a large fund-raising campaign was about to be announced, and several vice presidents had been added to Bok's staff. Harvard was also ready to build a new power plant for its medical school area in Boston, a study of the university's governance system was under way, and the faculty was set to debate a new undergraduate curriculum (the Core Curriculum). By the end of his first decade as president, Bok had put his stamp on so many aspects of Harvard that, had he retired then, his impact would have been felt far into the future. But he did not leave, despite his belief that ten years was about the right length of time in a university administrative job. Instead, as Harvard looked toward the celebration of its 350th birthday in 1986, Bok settled in more permanently, to see through some of the changes he had initiated, to refine and redefine some others, and to deal with a host of new problems that had materialized, partly as a result of the changes he had wrought.

From his Elmwood Avenue home to the parking garage in the basement of Holyoke Center is a distance of about one mile. Though he could drive in a university car or afford to buy himself something sporty or luxurious, Bok makes the trip in a red Volkswagen beetle. This symbolic parsimony typifies a man who seems to care so little about personal financial gain that he reportedly annoys his counterparts at Yale and Princeton because their annual salaries are set partly with Bok's as an example. Not until 1983–84 did his salary exceed $100,000, and it was still less than that of a few Harvard deans and professors and several of the highly paid professionals who manage Harvard's endowment; the year before that, Bok earned less than one of his own vice presidents. He never said anything publicly about this — no one at Harvard would ever commit such a vulgarity — but it is likely that he never said anything privately either. Once, when Bok and the dean of the Faculty of Arts and Sciences, Henry Rosovsky, had to travel to London on short notice, Rosovsky suggested they fly first class. Bok vetoed the idea. Business class would be sufficient. Other, poorer schools could waste their money on such vanities.

It is a short walk from the parking garage across Massachusetts Avenue into Harvard Yard and to Massachusetts Hall, and once indoors Bok is safe from strangers who stare as he passes, students who want to shake his hand. Far removed from the hectic atmosphere of Harvard Square, only a few hundred feet away, his cloistered headquarters are defined by elegant taste. Bok likes to greet his visitors personally, coming to the formal reception area to meet them. Leading a caller, who may feel more like a guest, down that hallway, introducing himself as they walk, as though the person doesn't know this is Bok, the president opens the door to his large office. The green carpet, off-white walls, fireplace, and modest accumulation of papers on the desk in the room's center contribute to a feeling of comfort. Absent is the technological accouterment of the modern executive, a computer. Oil paintings hang on the walls, near the red couch where Bok sits, spreading his arms wide behind him and placing his feet on the coffee table before him.

Like the institution he serves, Bok is afraid of being misunderstood, so much so that he even writes his own speeches. He speaks quietly, rarely hesitating. Dressed in a business suit, with a plain-collared shirt rather than the usual Harvard buttondown, he looks slightly uncomfortable, as though choosing his clothes is low on his list of interests. In a formal interview, he will answer all questions, but he bridles at those that smack of criticism, particularly of an answer he has just given. He says nothing about the weather or baseball or his family, nothing that might make conversation with him easier or more pleasant. Though his answers to some questions go on at length, he seems in a hurry to get them over with, and like the good labor lawyer he was trained to be, he isn't easily led into a cross-examination of what he has said or a revelation he doesn't intend. Seemingly incapable of false flattery or hyperbole, he tends toward the vocabulary of a statue when he's asked about his private life. He laughs frequently — short, sharp bursts of laughter, his entire face lighting up — and frequently the laughter is at himself. He listens intently, instantly grasping the direction of a question and sometimes, with barely controlled impatience, beginning his answer before the question has been completely stated.

Bok has impressed his colleagues with one of his grandfather's virtues, unpretentious hard work. He chairs every ad hoc committee himself, and by common consensus gives his greatest internal attention to appointing professors. His colleagues commend him on his ability to delegate minor jobs, "and he has a way of talking with you that is helpful without butting in," says one. Calvinistic, he reads all his mail and frequently replies with handwritten answers. He has never learned to dictate. On a plane

trip from Boston to Chicago, he might write twenty letters, all
in a clean, fluid hand, because he knows exactly what he wants
to say. Circumspect to the extreme in his dealing with the press,
which nevertheless reports his every major utterance, he keeps
much to himself. In his official vita, or résumé, which runs two
single-spaced pages and which includes a list of nine professional
affiliations and ten publications, he has placed "1971– President, Harvard University" at the beginning of the vita's first
category, labeled with lovely understatement as "Professional
Experience."

"Derek's a critic," says Dean Rosovsky. "He's not calculating.
He's not a performer. He has retained close relationships with his
friends from the old days." Bok has watched over Harvard, taken
care of it, Rosovsky believes. "He travels relatively little. He has
been a pastoral president."

Several years ago, Bok and Rosovsky were returning from
Paris with reservations on the same plane. When they arrived at
the ticket counter, the plane had just one seat left. Bok insisted
that Rosovsky take it, though Bok's family was already on the
plane. Eventually, both were accommodated. The memory of
the small incident still amazed Rosovsky, who couldn't believe
the president of Harvard — never mind his name, just think of
him as the holder of the most famous such office in the land —
could make such a gesture genuinely and without a fuss.

"Sometimes visitors to the university are surprised when I
pick them up at the airport," Rosovsky reports. "There are no
limousines at Harvard.

"You can't describe our jobs in simple terms," continues Rosovsky. "In certain spheres, Bok has enormous authority. In others, none. He's like the president of the United States in some
ways. He's a symbol, the head of one branch. He's the commander-in-chief, and the dean of the faculty is the field com-
mander with the biggest army. Though a university is far removed from the army, it's very hierarchical, without stripes on
the sleeves."

Borrowing from corporate terminology, Rosovsky asserts, "Bok is the CEO, at one level. At another, it's very different." Derek Bok, chief executive officer, Harvard University: the leader of one of the world's preeminent universities is a business executive — in one sense. But in another, not at all. He runs a business whose product lines are blurred with its finances, and his role is partly determined by that confusion.

Harvard finances, says Financial Vice President Thomas O'Brien, as if to ignore the labyrinth of his domain, "are deceptively simple. The deans have discretion over all income and expenses, but parameters are set within the budgetary process. I see summaries at the end of each fiscal year. There is a tremendous autonomy and discretion, but a lot of discussion with the chief academic officer, who is Derek Bok.

"You know," O'Brien says, "many college presidents get into trouble by telling faculty members one thing and students another." Obviously, he continues, specific details given to one group may not be the same emphasized to a different audience. But Bok, O'Brien says, "has taught us all: you tell the same story to everyone."

Referring to financial matters, over which he says the president shouldn't have to exercise himself, O'Brien confesses, "If you want to get the boss upset, tell him 'Don't worry about it.'" A "senior man" shouldn't have to work, O'Brien explains, sounding as though he were trying to convince himself. After more than a decade, O'Brien was still trying to figure out the man he called his boss.

Tufts '60, Cornell Ph.D. '69, and White House fellow '70, O'Brien is a career Harvard administrator, with the exception of a two-year interregnum in the mid-1970s in state government. Jovial, given to homilies about good works and good people, O'Brien believes without a blush that most of his Harvard colleagues feel the university is more important than their own concerns. "I've never had a discussion at Harvard that, if Harvard is better off, people don't go along." Then he adds, "That's one of the great pleasures of working here."

Many pecuniary pleasures brighten the world of this cordial, even-tempered master of Harvard's purse strings: the satisfaction of a balanced income statement each year, the conviction that the university's fund-raising success stems from donors' "deep care" for Harvard, the confirmation during fifteen happy years that people don't overspend their budgets. Of course there are nagging peculiarities, one of which, even with the help of computers, gives Harvard headaches. Departmental expenses are not matched, on a percentage basis, by departmental control of endowment. Two-thirds of Harvard's seventeen thousand students are enrolled within the Faculty of Arts and Sciences, but only about two-fifths of Harvard's endowment is controlled by the same giant "department." Harvard stresses this fact in its requests for unrestricted gifts to endowment, pointing out that a much smaller institution, with a much smaller endowment, may still have more endowment per student than does Harvard.

Looking forward one morning to a ten o'clock meeting with the Harvard Corporation during which he would present his annual report, O'Brien was especially contented. Tomorrow he was leaving for a conference in Puerto Rico, but the prospect of the beach and the ocean pleased him less than the recent successful refinancing of some bonds issued in Harvard's behalf a few years before. Harvard had just saved several million dollars in borrowing costs.

By early 1985, Harvard was carrying a debt of over $600 million. By far the largest such liability of any university in the United States, it would grow by another $140 million before the year was over. Many of the bonds that comprised this debt had been floated to pay the $370 million construction costs and interest charges for its Medical Area Total Energy Plant, which is the biggest single building project ever undertaken by an American university. Coincidentally, at around the time those bonds were refinanced, Harvard was concluding the Harvard Campaign to raise $350 million (though it was not the largest such university campaign in the country, it was the largest devoted primarily to undergraduate education). Harvard sets high standards in whatever it does — the highest in the world, O'Brien brags. The standards are in fact so high, he continues, that they "strip away your hubris," because when there is a problem at Harvard it gets great attention. The power plant, a diesel-power cogeneration facility commonly referred to as MATEP, was that kind of problem. Several years after its construction, it was still not in full use, its start-up mired in a lengthy regulatory process and numerous court cases. Harvard's South African investments was another such problem.

Only a small portion of Harvard's nontuition income is received for an actual service performed. Large chunks of cash come in with no strings attached. An alumnus or alumna gives Harvard a million dollars and has nothing tangible to show for it; except, in some cases, for the donor's name on a building, there is no formalized quid pro quo. Perhaps the donor will be nominated to be a director of the Harvard Alumni Association, but this is hardly the stuff dreams are made of. The major reward will come from the federal government in the form of a sizable tax deduction. The tension here is that without this kind of funding, Harvard would no longer be able to educate in the style to which it has become accustomed. Neither the funding nor the education would exist without the other, but the funding is given without guarantee that education commensurate with the amount of money will take place and with no direct benefit to the donor.

Several months after the end of its fiscal year, which goes from July 1 to June 30, Harvard publishes a document entitled *Financial Report to the Board of Overseers of Harvard College*. The report, which is now issued jointly by the treasurer and the financial vice president, comes in a soft-cover crimson package, and its nearly one hundred pages are filled with financial tables and easy-to-read charts. In the heyday of government grants, when tuition was reasonable and fund raising was an innocent marriage of artful appeal and traditional school spirit, the report attracted little attention, save from the small group of administrators and the two governing boards who ran Harvard.

Twenty years ago, the treasurer's report was still just a standard summary of Harvard's finances, of little interest to most people in the Harvard community and of none to the general public. Now, since Derek Bok's report as president has been transformed from a narrative history of the preceding academic year into an essay on a subject of educational concern, such as computer use, the treasurer's report has become the closest thing Harvard has to an annual record of the twelve months past. But none of the events reported is academic. Harvard's yearly account of itself is an annual corporate report, scrutinized by its vast, ever-growing bureaucracy. Fifteen years ago, Harvard's annual budget was less than $200 million. Now the figure exceeds $600 million, much of it to employ about twelve thousand people, including three thousand teachers.

Harvard's *Financial Report* for the fiscal year 1983–84, dated November 6, 1984, opened with a two-page preface that summarized the status of Harvard's finances as of June 30, 1984. Highlighted were a decrease of slightly over 5 percent in the value of the endowment, a concomitant decrease in the market value of the unit by which Harvard allocates the overall endowment to the many funds of which it is composed, and the receipt of over $125 million of gifts for capital, which was about the same as the year before. After a note on tuition and fees, total expenses and income, Harvard's general operating account, and MATEP, the substance of the report began immediately with an "Analysis of Financial Results," and throughout the rest of the document, which included the annual report of the Harvard Management Company, a special section on federally sponsored research, and thirty pages of financial statements, Harvard was human. Yet there was little indication in the even prose and the accompanying figures and charts that those who prepared the report realized this.

All the numbers in this pro forma record added up as they

were supposed to. But their message was also an admission by proud Harvard, which uses no limousines but on June 29, 1984, owned over 240,000 shares, with a market value of nearly $16 million, in the General Motors Corporation. Missing was the hauteur of an institution whose motto, Veritas, means truth but whose investment policies so provoke some of its professors and students that its president can be prevented from working in his own office. For Harvard to say it is "highly dependent" on tax-exempt bonds for "the upgrading of its facilities," for it to warn that "recent efforts in Congress to restrict universities' access to this market posed a special threat," was to eat humble pie. A suppliant now to strangers, Harvard had to range far from its large extended "family" for funds.

Accepting a gift or asking for another, Harvard can marshal figures to explain everything that affects its finances, from the impact of federal dollars for research — down in twenty years from one-third to one-fifth of the university's operating income — to the accelerating cost of supporting the acquisitions of the world's largest university library, which contains more than ten and a half million volumes. With so many figures from which to choose, Harvard can also make a case for anything it wants or thinks it ought to do, adopting whatever pose is appropriate to the argument. As one of the largest private landholders in Massachusetts, Harvard, despite its standing as a nonprofit institution — legally, in Massachusetts, a public charity — makes voluntary payments in lieu of taxes to municipalities in which it owns property. Some officials may grumble about the size of the payment (one Cambridge politician who has made a career of complaining about Harvard's calculated noblesse oblige has suggested taking Harvard Yard by eminent domain and paving it for public parking), but Harvard can cite a long list of numbers to prove the positive impact of its presence on the local economy. Variations on the same point — what Harvard does for others — are used when Derek Bok goes to Washington, where many of Harvard's former students also happen to be elected and appointed officials.

Harvard's largest annual expense by category is salaries and wages, accounting for over 44 percent of its budget in 1983–84, or nearly 53 percent when employee benefits are added in. Equipment and supplies accounted for 16.5 percent that year, scholarships for nearly 8 percent, and the remaining 23 percent went for space and occupancy charges, telephone service, travel, publications, consultants' fees, and the like. Harvard has maintained a balanced budget over the past decade, but endowment income and federal research funding have grown at a lower annual compound rate than expenses. The slack has been made up principally by increases in student tuition and fees and current gifts.

To control utility costs, Harvard has metered each of its buildings, so it knows how much electricity, water, and steam (for heat) they use. That knowledge informs such prudent decisions as where to invest in insulation. Harvard has its own audit department, which reports to Tom O'Brien, and an office that monitors expenditures for research funded by the federal government. Restricted funds — those that must be spent in specific areas — are also monitored, and O'Brien boasts that he's never run across an intentional error.

Forty-eight Harvard departments are assigned a total of ninety-five main accounts in the university's bookkeeping system. The Faculty of Arts and Sciences has several accounts, while most departments have just one. Major departmental accounts are divided into subdepartmental accounts; central administration has about one thousand of these, and overall there are approximately ten thousand. The accounts for the Faculty of Arts and Sciences, which includes the undergraduate college, comprise the largest item in Harvard's annual budget — over $183 million in 1983–84. Harvard spent less that year on the School of Dental Medicine, the Graduate School of Design, and the Divinity School, taken individually, than it did to run the company that manages its portfolio. Food services accounted for $14.5 million in 1983–84, the Harvard University Press over $9 million, Phillips Brooks House (a voluntary social service organization) a quarter of a million dollars. Total departmental expenses were nearly $710 million, but this figure was offset by about $123 million for interdepartmental transactions, a varying portion of which is represented in each of the figures cited above. Some of these charges were unusual; for example, the Faculty of Arts and Sciences "rents" office space in Massachusetts Hall to the central administration.

In its finances, Harvard follows an old Harvard monetary dictum, so ingrained in the life of the institution that it is identified by an acronym, ETOB. The practice has been both modified and, as Harvard admits, not uniformly enforced, but Harvard still subscribes to the financial notion that "every tub stands on its own bottom." In other words, each department at Harvard is an independent budgetary unit; Medical School tuitions cannot pay Law School professors, and the teaching of Sanskrit cannot be subsidized by the sale of football tickets. Moreover, each "tub" competes with the others, forcing an internal justification of every expense.

Because Harvard's monthly cash flow is so large — about one billion dollars — how checks are cleared and revenues deposited has an impact on the balance sheet. At Harvard, payments for student term bills go directly into a locked box at the Harvard Trust Company (not a Harvard affiliate). Trying to promptly deposit checks sent to Harvard for other reasons, Tom O'Brien points out, can be "a terrible problem." Donors make gifts in many ways, and a check to the Friends of Harvard Track, for example, may not be completely routed through the proper crediting channels for several days. Multiplied by many such donations, this kind of delay causes appreciable lost interest and dividend income.

"From a business view," a new Harvard dean said, "the way this place is organized — the structure, how decisions are made — plain looks funny." But it works. Still learning to operate within that structure, this dean scheduled his time by the half-hour slot in an appointment calendar that became, a month in advance, a dense mass of people's names and committee meetings and social occasions.

You could keep very active as a Harvard administrator, and no matter how much you farmed out, you could find more to do. Harvard now has its own in-house legal department, under the supervision of Vice President Daniel Steiner. The idea, according to former Harvard Corporation member Francis "Hooks" Burr, was to save Harvard some money, but like so many improvements the practice seems instead to have spawned further growth. Steiner is as busy as ever, and he keeps adding more lawyers, just as the alumni association adds more people to run new programs and the company that manages Harvard's endowment adds more investment professionals.

None of the people working for Harvard, with the exception of a few professionals at the Harvard Management Company, are getting rich. They work in Harvard's five hundred and fifty buildings, which are named Sever and Houghton, Wadsworth and Lowell, the names a kind of history of Harvard, a litany of Harvard benefactors and achievers. Even the vice presidents, whose average salary is $90,000, earn less than they might in business or private practice. Many professors and deans live comfortably, but the primary personal rewards are a sense of laboring for a greater good and the perks that come with the jobs (nice vacations, pleasant working conditions, a stimulating environment). Handling money, Harvard confronts a host of expectations and assumptions. Its billions are a hindrance as well as a help, and the institution is frequently a victim of its own success, unable to convince some of its constituents of its need. Harvard "ought to be in the business of making money any way that is legal," its treasurer for many years used to say. But Harvard's real business is education.

To have money is power; to talk about money is to dilute that power, to share it. Money means survival to some, growth to others; to Harvard it traditionally means independence. Harvard is a goose that lays golden eggs. Financially, it functions dynamically. Harvard spends money to make money. It runs an elaborate alumni association and a modern development office to raise funds from its alumni. Its budget includes over $7 million for a company to manage its portfolio. An elaborate two-tiered governance system makes decisions and sets policy for a huge bureaucracy overseen by a president, five vice presidents, and many more deans.

Even more than its reputation for intellectual excellence, Harvard's wealth invites the assumption that what goes on within its ivied walls must make sense. The heart of Harvard's social and political power is money, but an inquiry about the sources of that money is thwarted by taboo. Like the intricate arrangements for a leveraged buyout or the complicated maneuvers for a large commercial bank loan, Harvard's financial management is a game whose rules, if you don't already know them, you don't hear about. Money may talk, but no one inside Harvard is supposed to talk indiscreetly about money — at least not Harvard's. Though the subject is a constant preoccupation of anyone in a position of administrative authority, money is treated the way a life insurance company treats death. Just as that company's policies, in the printed words of its literature and the spoken appeals of its salespeople, sell security, so Harvard, in its requests for money, seeks to save the world. "Harvard," one of its fund-raising brochures boldly proclaims, "offers an opportunity, unique even among major universities, to achieve the greatest impact with every philanthropic dollar."

Such inspirational marketing language was not yet in vogue fifteen years ago, just before Bok took over, when a Pusey-appointed committee issued a thirty-five-page document called *Harvard and Money.* Dated 1970, it is revealing of the climate of the times, making such defensive statements as: "Certainly, the paper will fail to satisfy those few who believe that the best thing Harvard could do with its endowment would be to give it away to poor people, and the next best, to dump it in the Charles on the ground that Harvard is a servant of evil in an evil society and the sooner it goes out of business, the better." But there was more in the report's analysis, which reads today like a rough blueprint for much of what happened afterward.

Arguing that Harvard was not rich and that financial difficulties were ahead, the report recommended that Harvard's fund-raising apparatus be overhauled and, without suggesting a remedy, indicated that the day-to-day management of Harvard's portfolio was impossible to monitor. The most important sentence, its brevity belying its profundity, emphasized the interrelatedness of different financial actions. "Money-spending, money-raising, and money-management are not separable subjects." Financial phenomena are neither isolated nor static; everything is connected and dynamic.

Conflict between institutional means and ends at Harvard is denied by those who run Harvard. Yet within the university, an entire business operation separate from yet critical to the educational process has been growing rapidly. A product is not in itself the reason for this business's existence; there is no product, except the generation of money through alumni fund raising, endowment management, and innovative financing schemes. This business exists solely to make possible something altogether different, and that creates a tension: money for Harvard must never on the outside seem more important than education, while within the institution its pursuit is an urgent, constant goal, without which Harvard would not be Harvard. Many people assume Harvard will continue to thrive as a matter of course, but this assumption of inevitable success only exacerbates the problem, because people don't recognize it.

Down Boylston Street from Harvard Square, the old Harvard, the Harvard of Eliot House and its former master, Professor John H. Finley, who wore three-piece suits with a pocket watch and recited Virgil in Latin from memory, his voice sometimes breaking under the spell of the beautiful cadences and caesuras — that Harvard still stands, physically, thanks to several million dollars of tax-exempt bonds issued a few years ago in anticipation of gifts to the Harvard Campaign. Professor Finley, long retired, can still be glimpsed walking up the wide stone staircase to Widener Library, on his way to study number 746, while his beloved Eliot House, recently rewired and painted, its roof repaired, shares its corner of Cambridge with expensive new Charles Square condominiums and the Kennedy School of Government.

Boylston Street has been renamed John F. Kennedy Street, but many people still call it Boylston. The subway from Boston once ended by it, on the present site of the Kennedy School. The grassy park between the school and Memorial Drive is situated on the former subway yards, where the cars were maintained. The adjacent condominiums, luxury hotel, and shops form part of a $72 million commercial redevelopment of the Harvard Square area. Refurbished Eliot House, with its red brick façade, full-framed white windows, and cupola, looks endearingly out of place next to its trendy rich neighbors.

From an upper-story Eliot House window you can see across Memorial Drive and the Charles River to Harvard's sports complex. Eighteen million dollars of campaign money paid for improvements in the athletic facilities at a university that says it downplays the importance of sports. From the Olympic-size swimming pool to the outdoor track, everything earns state of the art status, except Harvard's policy toward intercollegiate competition. Here Harvard is ahead of the times, or behind them, depending on your point of view. No athletic scholarships, no NCAA Division I football. No dumb jocks; just coddled ones.

Money makes such a policy possible. If money can't buy love, it can certainly support the ideal of the scholar-athlete whose studies come first. Harvard doesn't need to pay its football players to fill Harvard Stadium for the Harvard-Yale game. They pay Harvard, as do several thousand other students, whose tuition buys them an appreciation of aesthetic beauty or the ability to think critically or the most important intangible of all, a Harvard degree. Operating in a seller's market, Harvard turns many others away at the gate, a huge group that would willingly fork over the orchestra-seat price for standing room, who wouldn't mind a little more crowding in the classroom and dormitory in return for a Harvard A.B. after their names. The result is called selective admissions. Money supports this ideal, too, much of it from alumni who view Harvard far more sentimentally than Harvard views them.

Selling Harvard

Marching up boylston street toward Harvard Square, W. Norton Grubb III put his trumpet to his lips and joined the other members of the Harvard University Band in a boisterous rendition of "Ten Thousand Men of Harvard." It was a late Saturday afternoon in September of 1965, and the band, dressed in their crimson coats and led by a huge bass drum, which was drawn along on a cart, was following its traditional route of parade after each home football game. Grubb, a 1965 graduate of Deerfield Academy, had the day before freshman registration driven to Harvard from Hanover, New Hampshire, where his stepfather was an Episcopalian priest. He expected mathematics to be his major — in Harvard parlance, his concentration.

Stuart Schoffman, Yeshivah of Flatbush '65, planned to concentrate in physics. Born and brought up in Brooklyn, New York, Schoffman combined a deep commitment to Judaism with a scholarly ambition inspired by the example of his father, a professor at Brooklyn College. Bilingual, Schoffman was earning a portion of his college expenses teaching Hebrew to young students at a temple in one of Boston's suburbs. Never a radical, he was nonetheless among the students who received an official warning from the university after turning in his university identification card as an onlooker at a demonstration in 1967.

That autumn afternoon in 1965, having attended morning services in observance of the Sabbath, Schoffman was in the stadium stands to see the game. So was Bruce G. Wilcox. The son of a Harvard administrator ("I grew up in the belly of the beast," he says), he'd been going to Harvard football games for as long as he could remember. Choate '65, Wilcox had stated in his registration forms, in the blank space next to the word *concentration,* "undecided." Not until he had to did he finally decide on economics, not an unuseful preparation for an eventual career in book publishing.

Harvard's Class of 1969 was greeted in September of 1965 by the dean of freshmen, F. Skiddy Von Stade Jr., who wrote in his introduction to a picture book of their faces, a hardbound crimson-colored volume called *The Freshman Register:*

> College education puts much more responsibility on the student, but there are a *lot* of knowledgeable people in the administration and faculty who are both interested and, most of the time, available. . . .
> Any freshman — indeed any student — should know, or must learn, that part of his responsibility is to ask questions. They won't always be answered to his satisfaction, but they won't be answered at all if he doesn't ask them.

Four years later, in a photograph published in a supplement to the Harvard yearbook, *Three Thirty Three,* Dean Von Stade was pictured in the grasp of a student who was evicting him from University Hall, which had been occupied by student protesters on April 8, 1969. On the facing page, President Pusey, speaking of the protesters, whom police had in turn evicted on Pusey's orders, was quoted:

> They did not intend to bargain. They ignored an adverse vote of their adherents in occupying the building. They ignored orders

to leave. They were prepared to barricade the building and to resist attempts at entry.

It was quite clear that the issue was a direct assault upon the authority of the university and upon rational processes and accepted procedures.

By the spring of 1969, the Harvard campus was so politicized by debate over the Vietnam War and other issues that it was difficult to converse with anyone without speaking at some point about the war. The same thing had been happening at colleges and universities across the country, and at Harvard the strike of 1969 was preceded by a series of similar events on a smaller scale and of a lesser magnitude. The occupation of University Hall was unexpected by most people in the Harvard community, and reaction to it and the police bust that followed early the next morning was deep and disruptive. Nothing in the rhetoric of the day indicated that exactly ten years after this discordant moment in Harvard's history the university would embark on its most ambitious fund-raising drive, asking former student radicals for money. To forgive is more than divine; it is profitable.

Sixteen pages of the prospectus for the Harvard Campaign were devoted to an illustrated time chart called "Harvard Through the Years." The earliest century in Harvard's history was summarized in less than one page, while the 1960s and 1970s each were given two pages. Next to a black and white photograph from that era, a boxed caption read: "A crowd of demonstrators and onlookers blocks Secretary of Defense Robert McNamara after a meeting with students. The incident is the first in a series of 'confrontations' culminating in the student occupation of University Hall in April 1969." Below the photograph, the single reference to 1967 non-Harvard history said, "U.S. troops in Vietnam are increased to 525,000."

When the Harvard Campaign solicited Bruce Wilcox fifteen years after his graduation, he was the director of the University of Massachusetts Press in Amherst, Massachusetts. Wilcox had by then spent two years in Africa as a Peace Corps volunteer, lived in New York City, Bangladesh, and Seattle, Washington, and taken up golf as a complement to soccer, which he'd played in college on a house team.

Economics became Norton Grubb's concentration, too — and the focus of his career. Married before his graduation to a Radcliffe student, Erica Black, Grubb returned to Cambridge in 1970 after teaching public school in Baltimore for one year, and his wife attended Harvard Law School while he completed a Ph.D. in economics in just five years. In 1984, they were living with their son and daughter in Austin, Texas, where Grubb was an associate professor at the L.B.J. School of Public Affairs at the University of Texas. He was the author of two books, including *Broken Promises: How Americans Fail Their Children,* a radical analysis of public schooling in the United States. They had not made a contribution to the Harvard Campaign, but he and his wife gave regularly to Radcliffe.

Stuart Schoffman no longer kept kosher, though his parents and one of his two brothers had moved to Israel, where Schoffman frequently visited. A former staff writer for *Time* and *Fortune,* Schoffman had abandoned his intention to become a college professor after earning a master's degree in history in 1972 from Yale. "Making an amusing living writing unproduced screenplays of improving caliber in various genres," he wrote in the 261-page *Fifteenth Anniversary Report* — for which members of the class were asked to contribute $25. Some class members balked at this; unaware that part of the money went toward subsidy of the Office of Class Reports, where several Harvard employees worked exclusively on the editing and production of these remarkable documents, they were put off by this indirect request for a further gift.

"Sit all day in shorts at a word processor," Schoffman continued, "in small rented aerie with postcard view of Pacific. Appreciating Los Angeles to the max, after nearly six years of resistance. . . . Casually planning play and novel on Important Themes with substantial intellectual content to be written for love not money. Long ago a child groom, divorced for a decade now, finally learning to enjoy the solitude even while dreaming of its surcease. Seeking Cliffie into Willie Nelson, Proust, and aerobics."

Fifteen years, almost to the day, after the events of the spring of 1969, the following invitation was mailed to all members of the class: "Our Fifteenth Reunion is practically here! From the enthusiasm we've heard from the 15th Reports, we all feel this is going to be our best reunion ever. We expect a terrific turnout from across the country — a great chance to catch up on old friends and make new ones."

Mary Blue Magruder was serving Harvard as co-chairperson of her class's Fifteenth Reunion Committee. Discussing the class — now the Harvard and Radcliffe Class of 1969 — Magruder mentioned an article in *Life* magazine a few years back about "the radicals": where were they now? Just recently, *Boston* magazine had run a piece on how "the radicals who stirred Harvard to bloodshed are now quiet citizens approaching middle age." It was a favorite media subject.

"So many changes in the last five years have been beneath the surface." Blue Magruder reported in the 1969 class's *Fifteenth Anniversary Report,* "I'm still at EARTHWATCH, but I've had the satisfaction of seeing this nonprofit triple in size. My work has taken me to dig mammoths in South Dakota, to explore Aboriginal rock art in Australia, and to climb through walled castles in Yemen. And I've now conquered my fear of giving talks at Rotary Clubs. . . . I enjoy life in Cambridge, weekends on the Cape, lots of sailing, good conversation with friends. I've found myself taking on many Harvard/Radcliffe and community responsibilities — including cochairing a committee on Joint 25th Reunions for the HAA [Harvard Alumni Association] and serving as a Regional Director of the RCAA [Radcliffe College Alumnae Association] — as well as work with the Boston Committee on Foreign Relations and the College Cevenol. The next five years will bring big decisions and changes . . . but I'll think about that tomorrow!"

With the full integration of Radcliffe and Harvard in the mid-1970s, there has been some confusion in the planning of reunion activities for many classes, Magruder said. Radcliffe continues to exist as a corporate and institutional entity. It has its own endowment, fund-raising programs, and trustees. Some have suggested this is because so many of Radcliffe's most generous donors are elderly and would not make contributions directly to Harvard. Radcliffe owns thirty-eight buildings, and it runs programs in women's studies, directs several institutes, and awards a number of fellowships, but in a complex bookkeeping arrangement, much of its $30 million annual budget goes to Harvard to pay for women's tuition, room and board, and financial aid.

"You know," Magruder said, "this is supposed to be a kind of watershed year for us. I mean, that's how Harvard looks at it. We've been out of school for a while now, and Harvard believes you can tell who's going to make it and who isn't."

Few members of the Class of 1969, whose number also included a U.S. senator and a movie star, attended their fifteenth reunion — but the real "watershed year" for the class was ten years away, in 1994. Meanwhile, a new generation of Harvard students, whose own major reunions would not take place until after the millennium, continued their education, which Harvard invited alumni to observe under highly staged circumstances.

Harvard alumni from all classes reconvene every June, the largest groups called "the fives" — those who graduated from the college five, or any multiple of that magic number, years before. They come from all parts of the country and overseas, sometimes alone but usually with spouses and children, and the largest group of all are the twenty-fives. Over five hundred members of the Harvard Class of 1959, plus their families, attended their twenty-fifth reunion in 1984, and Harvard put on a big bash for them, five days and four nights of carefully planned activities culminating in commencement. When this week-long adult camp was over, Harvard was several million dollars richer, counting all the campaign gifts that the class had contributed since the re-

union was just a date on a calendar several years before. The fee
— not to be confused with each individual's campaign contribution — was $559 per alumnus and family. Many campaign
contributions were much greater.

The Class of 1959 contributed almost $5 million to the Har-
vard Campaign, setting a record for twenty-fifth reunion giving.
A new such record is set almost every year. Eighty-four percent
of the class gave or made pledges to the campaign. The Class of
1924, celebrating its sixtieth reunion, gave $12 million; 84 per-
cent of the surviving members of that class contributed, including John L. Loeb, who made a $7.5 million gift to endow fifteen
junior faculty positions. Loeb also gave $1.5 million to the Grad-
uate School of Design. A total of over $30,000 was given by
about two-thirds of the nearly fifteen hundred graduating students in the Class of 1984, while the rebellious Class of 1969
barely hit the million-dollar level; the only pre-1970 Harvard
classes with lower totals were 1910, 1911, 1912, 1913, 1915,
1916, and 1917.

Long before alumni returned for reunion, they preened in
print for themselves and Harvard. "Sixty-three and one-half percent of us are married to our first wives," the Class of 1959 reported to itself, in an informally annotated statistical document
it published.

One of us has been down the metaphorical aisle four times —
surely the triumph of hope over experience. One of us, not the
same person, has moved twenty-five times since 1959.

We aren't particularly rich. For every one of us who makes
$250,000 or more per year another makes less than $30,000.
Happily, the low earners seem no less content with life, with a
few sad but honest exceptions peeking through. Twelve percent
of us are millionaires. . . .

While . . . many thought the request for favorite books and
movies was stupid, outrageous, or worse, fortunately, enough less
judgmental fun-loving types responded. You tell us your favor-
ites: *War and Peace* nips the Bible in a photo finish. *The Brothers
Karamazov* and *Moby Dick* run strong. . . .

Only thirty-seven percent call our health excellent. About one-half of us exercise regularly. Only one in five weighs what he did at Harvard and you can be sure only a handful weigh less. Almost two-thirds drink as much or more as we did at our twentieth reunion.

Three-quarters of the class are non-smokers and almost half of them are people who quit the vile weed. . . . Nearly two-thirds of us have never smoked a joint and drugs play no significant part for over ninety percent of the class. Over eighty percent have never had a tranquilizer. Few of us think drugs or alcohol are serious threats to our society.

Classmates could also peruse the *Twenty-fifth Anniversary Report,* a 943-page hardbound volume of classmate autobiographies. A treasury of anecdote and opinion, confession and pontification, the bulky book portrayed the class as basically a happy lot. "In many ways I've never left Harvard," wrote John D. Spooner, chairman of the Class of 1959's reunion executive committee.

"I've tried to insulate myself from the real world as much as Cambridge insulated most of us from too much reality," Spooner continued.

How has this been possible? I've been in the investment business since college, the greatest Alice in Wonderland game of them all. Every time that arena threatened to be more than fantasy, I wrote a book. With this schizophrenic life I've been lucky to never be too far away emotionally from the soft fantasy I remember walking through the Yard on a spring night with Bach or the Everly Brothers spilling out of hundreds of windows. Nothing has really changed in twenty-five years. Only the fads and the perception of change. Human nature chugs along in the same patterns. But perhaps there is less understanding of human nature today because it seems that, in most places in America, our children are not taught history any more.

Our college class always seemed to me to share a certain sense of humor, a detachment from the throng. We were observors, wryly passing judgment, not good at joining mass movements but almost insisting upon operating alone. We were a class with a strong sense of irony and, as I observe us, a sense that history deserves this ironic look.

David Dearborn '59, a professional Harvard fund raiser and his class's secretary, listed his goals: "short term — to see two sons in good colleges, to help Harvard raise its targeted $350 million, to see a record 590 classmates at our 25th. . . . Longer term — to see three children grow to be all they can be, for all of us to hold on to our physical and mental well-being in a world at peace, and to retire to enjoy the golf course, my stamp collection, my library, to see a bit more of the world, and to hear Mary sing to our grandchildren." For Nathaniel Saltonstall Howe Jr., a banking executive who lives in Greenwich, Connecticut, "life continues its hectic pace. Isabelle and I will celebrate our twentieth wedding anniversary next week. . . . The twins are away at boarding school. . . . I only wish the passage of time would slow down a bit so that all of us could enjoy it even more."

Twenty-six pages long, the official program for the twenty-fifth reunion of the Class of 1959 pictured on its cover a caricature of John Harvard in the recruiting pose of Uncle Sam, and underneath his pointing finger were the words BIG BROTHER WANTS YOU. It was 1984, and this was the program's only reference, indirect or otherwise, to George Orwell. Inside the program, mailed to alumni before the reunion, was information on Alcoholics Anonymous ("On Sunday, June 3, at 9:00 P.M. there will be a meeting of all AA members in Wadsworth House, Harvard Yard. At that time you may wish to schedule other meetings during the Reunion"); what to wear ("Cambridge can be warm, cold or in between in June. Be prepared for rain, as well. Dress for the entire week is informal with a few exceptions. Suggestions are made for what to wear at each event in the Program section of the guide. It is by no means to be considered 'required' dress, but is an attempt to respond to the many queries we receive regarding what is considered appropriate for the various occasions"); and maid service ("During the Reunion week maid service will be limited to daily lavatory service and emptying the trash. Five towels will be provided for each person at the beginning of the week. If at some time during the Reunion further

service is required, contact the house superintendent or phone
————. Please place trash outside the door prior to 9:00 A.M.").

On Monday morning of reunion week, by the door to the auditorium in the Science Center, where President Bok and Dean
Rosovsky spoke to a standing-room-only crowd of alumni, a table had been prominently placed for the Harvard/Radcliffe Endowment for Divestiture Education Committee. On the table
was a flyer announcing a panel discussion the next night called,
"The $400 Million Question: Should Harvard Divest from
South Africa?" Next to the flyers was a stack of photocopies of a
single-page circular, "Brief Answers for Complex Questions on
the Endowment for Divestiture." Inside the auditorium, President Bok devoted a portion of his remarks to the many recent
changes in Harvard's physical facilities made possible in part by
the Harvard Campaign. Warm applause greeted the president,
and throughout his address, as he recited a long list of institutional accomplishments, Bok introduced each fact with the pro-
noun *we*.

That evening, an hour before conductor Harry Ellis Dickson
walked onto the stage of Symphony Hall in Boston, a large con-
tingent of uniformed Boston police officers waited outside to direct traffic when the school buses carrying twenty-fifth reunion
classmates and their families arrived for Harvard 25th Reunion
Night at the Boston Pops. Soon, seated at tables on the main
floor of the hall, concert-goers ("dresses, long skirts, jackets and
slacks are appropriate") sipped Pops Punch and Taittinger, Brut
La Française, while listening to orchestral arrangements of *Clair
de Lune,* by Debussy-Mouton-Piston, *Little Fugue in G-minor,*
by Bach-Cailliet, and *Tuxedo Junction* by Hawkins-Miller-Hay-
man. The stage was lit in red-and-white rectangles and squares
of light bulbs, and there were fresh flowers in front of the podium. Dickson, a graduate of the New England Conservatory of
Music, wore a crimson coat.

Shortly before 11 A.M. on reunion week's Essex Day (Tuesday
to the rest of the world), David Dearborn was standing next to

the tenth tee of the Essex County Club's golf course looking for a match. Heavy rains the week before had until almost the last moment jeopardized the golf (portions of the course were still very wet) and it was hot out: not ideal conditions for trooping about these lovingly cared-for greens and gently rolling fairways near the sea in Manchester. Wearing a sport shirt, crimson pants, and sneakers, Dearborn was sucking on a sourball — he had a pocketful in his pants, because he'd just quit smoking — as one of his classmates, a dentist from Michigan, reported his golfing handicap was only nine. "I usually don't break one hundred," confessed Dearborn, a member of the even more exclusive Myopia Hunt Club in nearby Hamilton. After he put his drive on the tenth in some water, he added, "I'm taking a lesson this weekend." The tenth tee is adjacent to the practice green, and adjacent to that an enormous yellow-and-white-striped tent had been erected for the reunion clambake. ("Tuesday, June 5, 5:30–7:00 P.M. Cocktails and New England Clambake. Please take only one lobster.")

So much to do — even for the children, who were divided by age into groups called Blue, Orange, Green, Red, and Grape (the last being the youngest). Kids and parents alike went on field trips. One of the grownups' optional excursions was a tour of the John Fitzgerald Kennedy Library. This memorial to the thirty-fifth president of the United States, which was originally to have been connected with Harvard, is located at Columbia Point, which juts into Boston Harbor beyond the Boston campus of the University of Massachusetts. The library was built there because of concerns in Cambridge about the potential for traffic congestion. There is no parking problem at Columbia Point, where a yellow school bus filled with fifty-niners pulled into the lot the morning of Essex Day (they were not permitted to drive their own cars on reunion field trips). After leaving here, alumni reboarded their school bus for the hour-long drive to the Essex County Club, where some of their classmates were already playing tennis or golf.

On Wednesday evening of reunion week, while most of the Class of 1959 danced to the music of Lester Lanin's orchestra at the Marriott Hotel, the Harvard Glee Club and the Harvard University Band gave a joint concert on the steps of Memorial Church. Admission was free, and there was a good crowd, though the thousands of empty chairs set up for the next day's commencement festivities made the number of people present seem smaller. The concert concluded with the singing of Harvard songs, and alumni were invited to the stage to join in. The last selection was "Fair Harvard," written for Harvard's 1836 bicentennial by Samuel Gilman, Class of 1811.

> Fair Harvard! thy sons to thy jubilee throng.
> And with blessings surrender thee o'er.
> By these festival rites, from the age that is past
> To the age that is waiting before.
>
> O relic and type of our ancestors' worth
> That has long kept their memory warm,
> First flower of the wilderness! star of their night!
> Calm rising through change and through storm!

"I had a problem, not with vision, but with understanding the world around me."

Psychiatrist and Harvard professor Robert Coles, the author of numerous articles and many books, including the monumental *Children of Crisis* series, was speaking to alumni Wednesday morning during one of several symposiums scheduled that week. On this lovely, warm day, Coles had taken off his jacket and rolled up the sleeves of his blue workshirt.

The title of Coles's talk was "The Moral Life of the Young." Much of it was taken from material in the first volume of *Children of Crisis,* published in 1967. This was not the first time Coles had addressed a forum of fellow alumni. The Harvard Alumni Association sponsors a speakers' program, in which Harvard professors and administrators are sent around the country as the featured guests at local Harvard affairs. Already, in 1983–84, Coles had spoken for Harvard in Minneapolis/St. Paul, St.

Louis, New Orleans, and Houston, making him one of the most traveled stars on the circuit. Coles's speech was delivered without notes, and it lasted about one hour; though he prefers not to take questions from the floor, two were permitted this day, and his answers lasted about twenty minutes each. Afterward, many in the audience introduced themselves to Coles, and almost another hour passed before he was able to keep a luncheon engagement with a student. Never, during this nearly three-hour-long performance, did he betray impatience or boredom; nor, even during the most fleeting exchange with an alumnus as he was leaving, did Coles cease to animate what he said or register what he heard with facial expressions that mirrored his emotion.

After noting that his wife had graduated from Radcliffe the same year — 1959 — as most of the alumni present, Coles quickly plunged into the substance of his subject, which he stated as "radical moments in history which cause us to look at our own assumptions." Ranging in his historical and literary references from Dietrich Bonhoeffer to William Faulkner, Coles recalled a lecture by the late Harvard professor Perry Miller about Bonhoeffer. Quoting Miller, who Coles said was quoting Reinhold Niebuhr, Coles continued, "It is very hard to know what one is to do with one's assumptions when confronted with someone such as Bonhoeffer," the theologian who chose during World War II to leave the United States to return to Germany and face certain death (he was executed by the Nazis just before the war ended). Coles had been speaking for only five minutes, but there was now not another sound in the packed auditorium.

Soon, Coles was narrating an experience of personal awakening in Mississippi in 1960, when, as a young psychiatrist in the air force, he chanced upon an ugly racial scene on the "beautifully maintained sands of a federal beach." That scene turned on the use of the beach by blacks; Coles's narrative of the scene turns on his realization that his own assumptions as a New England–bred, Harvard-educated physician, living and working in the pre–civil rights movement South, were being challenged.

Coles chose to remain in the South after his military service was completed, and he spent considerable time in New Orleans, which was undergoing the court-ordered desegregation of its public schools. Coles and his wife came to know the black children who were at the center of this crisis; he met their families; and he talked with teachers and others whose lives were being affected by this "radical moment in history."

The talk reached its climax when Coles recalled a six-year-old girl named Ruby, who moved her lips without making sounds as she walked each day into her school, while a crowd outside insulted her and threatened her life. "Father, forgive them, for they know not what they do," she was saying. And then Coles jumped from Ruby to Ralph Waldo Emerson's address "On Character," and then back to Perry Miller, and Coles said to the people "in this room, this hall, this college" — the rhetorical flourishes multiplying as he came to his conclusion — that "what makes Harvard great" is that "men such as Perry Miller taught there, *here*."

One of the two questions that followed concerned Harvard's investment in companies that do business in South Africa. At that time, the university estimated that about $400 million of its endowment was invested in such companies. After mentioning that he was completing the research for a book about South Africa, Coles articulated his own ambivalence about divestment. He said he sometimes wished that the students who put so much effort into the protest against such investments "would spend half that energy doing something in the community of Cambridge." This remark was loudly applauded. Then Coles noted the illusion that divestment would rid the institution of the question, and called for an awareness that "the problems of South Africa are our problems."

Many months later, as Coles was writing his book, he feared that the situation in South Africa "was about to flare up" — in that country and in the United States. He commented on a report that, during a four-hour visit to Cambridge, South African bishop Desmond M. Tutu, winner of the 1984 Nobel Peace

Prize, had been unable to meet with President Bok, because of conflicts in their schedules. "Wasn't that something," Coles said, letting the remark go with his typical irony and wonder. He was, he said, soon going again on the alumni lecture circuit, to Fort Lauderdale and Phoenix. "Picking up vibes," he called it.

"I frankly enjoy it," Coles continued. "I meet more and more of the parents of my students, and sense the relationship between teaching students and the response to that in the hearts and minds of their families.

"[Professor] David Riesman talked to me about this a long time ago — about what he called 'the Harvard tribe.' And it keeps me in touch with a segment of American life." Recalling with some amusement a talk he had given a year or two before to the New York City Harvard Club, which had also invited fellow alumnus Norman Mailer to speak with him, Coles said no pressure was put on him by Harvard to make these appearances. To alumni, however, his participation lent credence to Harvard's appeals, adding to the fund-raising alchemy by which memory becomes money.

Over a third of the university's operating income comes from gifts for current use and a portion of endowment income, and the major source of these funds is Harvard's alumni body of over 200,000 people. To get those alumni in the habit of giving, to keep them thinking of Harvard's needs as a constant in their own lives, Derek Bok leaves his ivory tower often. But he doesn't like it. If talking about money is distasteful, having to ask for it is humiliating. Bok, of course, can always justify this part of his job as a way of staying in touch with alumni, of learning what they think about Harvard. But the real purpose of his talks to alumni gatherings, his correspondence with prominent alumni, and his travels around the country to meet selected donors is to pay the piper.

With a major fund-raising drive under way, Harvard had modernized its alumni association. By the time the campaign was over and Harvard was preparing to commemorate its 350th anniversary, its relations with alumni had taken on a new dimension. Harvard officials and volunteer fund raisers stressed that Harvard is now in better touch with its alumni. But that change was trivialized by advertisements for the *Harvard Magazine* 1986 "350th Anniversary Calendar" ("in keeping with the occasion, we bring you a calendar that, as the days pass, lets you recapture time" — for only $8.95).

Not until they are alumni do most students have occasion to stop at the office of the alumni association. None of them, save for the occasional enterprising reporter for the student newspaper, knows its director. Nameless others keep alumni happy about Harvard, but giving them an illusion of importance that goes beyond dollars and cents taxes Harvard's creativity and energy. Its graduates — like good uncles, distant, benevolent, and rich — are also a notoriously independent lot, and they aren't above criticizing alma mater. With a shake of the head and a sigh, in the manner of a cleric lamenting one of the flock's loss of faith, university officials call this Harvard-bashing. Even if he wanted to, Derek Bok couldn't attend to every one of Harvard's wayward sheep, nor feed and reward all the obedient ones. This task has been assigned to a chargé d'affaires.

The executive director of the Harvard Alumni Association, David Aloian, conveys the impression of an individual for whom there is no distinction between private life and institutional career. A solicitous man whose thinning, almost white hair is in sharp contrast to his dark, thick eyebrows and whose deep-set eyes focus with intensity on his many visitors, Aloian has never lost the fatherly mannerisms he must have learned when he was a prep school headmaster. Exuding warmth and well-meaning in his second-floor office at Wadsworth House, where he supervises a staff of thirteen, he has cultivated a gracious, personal demeanor, all the while tenaciously guarding the gates of Harvard, to which he clearly feels a special allegiance.

As well as directing the alumni association, Aloian is also president of the Harvard Club of Boston and master of Quincy

House, one of the student residences. This latter title, which requires that he and his wife live in the master's suite at Quincy, suits the personality of an alumnus who truly seems to have come home to Harvard. Completely comfortable whether discussing the alumni association budget, over which he exercises considerable authority, or reminiscing about alumni he has known — one imagines him in the style of Will Rogers insisting he's never met one he didn't like — Aloian has so identified himself with Harvard's cause he seems unaware there could be any other.

Though the Harvard Alumni Association was not overseeing Harvard's $350 million campaign, everything it did primed the campaign pump. The reunions the association ran, the alumni weekends and workshops it organized, and the inescapable Harvard presence it placed in its members' lives, all converged on the campaign. Choosing his words carefully one day near the beginning of the campaign's final year, Aloian delivered himself of a Harvard homily:

"The campaign's success . . . all flows actually in the life of this place and the commitment of the alumni to it, the deep feelings of alumni for decades. And for reasons one can't understand, something goes out of here and affects a person, generates some pride and gratitude, generates a gift; but you don't always know what it is. The campaign is a stunning statement about that."

Aloian's brown loafers matched the brown in his herringbone jacket. No one working in an administrative position at Harvard wears clothing that could be mistaken for the attire of an athlete or an actor. The emphasis, if it could be called that, is on comfort, and the effect is one removed from the proper, conservative image of the executive in a major corporation. Flair is frowned on, but an identification with academia is cultivated: no turtlenecks, but something more than a white shirt and a plain suit.

"There are probably ten — no, make it twenty — administrators here who among themselves know just about every Harvard alumni leader in the world," said Aloian. "Their active memories are one of our best resources." The sentences flowed freely;

Aloian was warming to his subject. "In a way, Harvard is organized like General Motors, with a central financial control and a decentralized administration. . . . You don't feel someone else is influencing you, which creates self-respect — you're not just carrying out at the lower level. Many people like their work here."

David Aloian likes his very much. The alumni association he directs manages a wide variety of activities, many of them organized through sixteen standing committees. They include such groups as an alumni awards committee, an overseers-directors nominating committee, and a "happy observance of commencement committee." There are no dues to join the association; automatic membership, in fact, is one of the few things Harvard offers its alumni at no charge. With an annual budget of about $700,000, the Harvard Alumni Association "can be viewed," its orientation handbook states, "as an 'alumni Senate,' representing the views of alumni to Harvard, and Harvard's views, needs, and policies to its constituencies."

For some alumni, their involvement in the association is a steppingstone to becoming an overseer. Aloian used the word *arena* in talking about this, but he insists there is only "minimal" self-promotion at work, despite some competition among members for status within the association.

"Harvard people seem to develop a strong feeling about Harvard, not always laudatory. The level of concern is impressive. Past scholarship holders want to pay Harvard back. . . . Many firms encourage pro bono work. Harvard clubs, such as the one in New York — a magnificent facility — are a great way for young alumni to make connections with established alumni."

The twenty-fifth reunion class has been going to Essex for at least twenty years, according to Aloian. On second thought, he amended his answer and said the day has been "one of several standard items" since the mid-fifties. The Pops concert is another; so are the dance and the opening night dinner.

There are, he continued, variations on smaller reunion matters from class to class. The class reunion committee is in place two years before its reunion. The leaders — five or six of them — attend the preceding twenty-fifth reunion. There are discussions about what the program will be, but not about "the pillars."

There is not a lot of information about who does and does not come. Where a person lives has something to do with that decision, said Aloian, and so does occupation. "Those in teaching are, perhaps, less willing to invest a whole week." Reunion and commencement week used to take place later in June, but "holding seniors here was a problem. It was less popular and less cohesive. Harvard mailed many diplomas."

The class reports go back to the nineteenth century and are "one of the cornerstones . . . a valuable resource to keep the class together." They are used in "countless" ways — for example, in finding "individuals who might make good candidates for visiting committees and overseers," though the "standard information Harvard usually has. The twenty-fifth is a real catch-up. People seem more willing to talk about themselves." Alumni who write on the occasion of their tenth reunion say they are "busy as hell"; those writing on their twenty-fifth "have had a good life"; on their fiftieth they "are proud of Bill."

Because the number of alumni association directors is large, the whole is broken into small groups, which meet separately. Three times a year, all ninety directors come to Cambridge, and attendance is "excellent." In the fall, about ninety club presidents join the directors at one of those three annual meetings.

"Fifteen generations of graduates," the association's handbook concludes in crafted prose, "have built the Harvard we know today. Each generation, while fully savoring the Harvard of its own time, has been concerned with the Harvard to come and has endeavored to ensure its future. The HAA is a major partner in the always exciting and always rewarding enterprise of building the next Harvard." In another of the grand understatements that characterize Harvard's own literature about itself, the purpose of the alumni association is summarized as "the promotion of the welfare of Harvard University and the establishment of a mutually beneficial relationship between Harvard University and its Alumni." So civilized are its stated purposes that a stranger to private higher education in the United States might miss the message to alumni: your account with Harvard isn't squared.

"How do today's Harvard courses measure up to those of the past? Has dining hall food improved in recent years? What are the 'hot' issues confronting students?" These and other questions were the lead to a flyer promoting a "Return to Harvard Day," sponsored by the Harvard Alumni Association two months before reunion. The flyer was sent to members of fifth-year reunion classes in the Boston area, but any alumnus or alumna and his or her spouse and high-school-age children were welcome to attend, for the token price of $2 each (luncheon extra). Over three dozen regularly scheduled Harvard College classes were open to visitors, and a panel discussion, "Undergraduate Life Today," was the afternoon feature, followed by cocktails.

Registering for the day in the Senior Common Room of Lehman Hall, alumni were given name tags on which was printed a small silhouette of the Daniel Chester French statue of John Harvard that stands outside University Hall in the center of Harvard Yard. They could help themselves to free copies of the official weekly paper, *The Harvard University Gazette,* and a catalog of courses offered by the Center for Lifelong Learning. Then it was off to class, where alumni could sample Harvard's educational product.

The hallway by Sever Hall 113 was crowded just before noon. A bell rang, the door opened, and the students from a class taught by Professor Thomas Schelling exited, while those in the hallway began to enter the gray and white amphitheater-like lecture room. A minute later, a man in a camel-hair coat, scarf, and light brown felt hat strode down the short center aisle and ascended a staircase to a small stage. This man was Professor Donald Fleming, who now carefully took off his outer garments and neatly placed them over the balustrade that went across the front of the stage. Elegantly dressed in a dark blue jacket, gray slacks, a light blue shirt with a white collar, and a red tie (Windsor knot), he spoke briefly with a student, then erased the blackboard behind him and wrote on it, in large capital letters, which he underlined: "Counter-cultures and student rebellions."

Opening a brown leather briefcase, Professor Fleming set it on its side, so it formed a large V, facing him, and on top of this he placed a folder that held his lecture notes. He took his watch off and put it beside the notes. Then he peered through his glasses around the rapidly filling room, cleared his throat, blew his nose, watched silently while his graduate assistants wrote notes on the blackboard about their office hours, took off his glasses and cleaned them with a handkerchief, looked up as the room quieted, and at precisely 12:10 P.M. began the day's lecture with a reference to Freud's *Civilization and Its Discontents*.

Singing his phrases, each syllable of each word enunciated clearly, the voice varying in pitch for emphasis, with an extra inflection at the end of an especially important phrase, Fleming spoke for exactly fifty minutes without one stutter, one word taken back or amended, one unintended pause. Moving quickly to the work of C. Wright Mills, he referred to a well-known American university that, through Mills, might be perceived as "a kind of service station for the establishment." This brought the first of many laughs from his students, only one of whom was also wearing a coat and tie. Soon, Fleming was talking about Jack Kerouac and his "identification with the landscape." Kerouac, in some of his landscape passages, was "a hazy Thoreau." More laughs. Aldous Huxley was verbally impaled with a quoted passage about an "ineffable experience" Huxley said he had had with his flannel pants while he was on mescaline. And Timothy Leary: "once ensconced at Harvard . . . bound to be expelled as a foreign body." As Fleming continued this highly opinionated tour of alternative thinkers (pronouncing the first syllable of *alternative* as in the name *Al*), he often moved his hands like a conductor, while almost dancing on his feet from one side of the stage to the other. Once, he stepped back from his notes and made a long aside about Herbert Marcuse, and even here he didn't miss a word. He reached the climax of his lecture, marrying references to Marcuse and John Maynard Keynes, just as the bell rang, and his last words were followed by applause.

Seated at round tables in Harvard Hall, the largest room in the Harvard Club of Boston's main clubhouse on Commonwealth Avenue in Boston, over two hundred members and spouses attended its 1984 annual dinner meeting in March. The meal, which included filet mignon with Hollandaise sauce, cost $16.50 per person, though no cash or credit cards were accepted; charges were put on accounts. Dinner was preceded by cocktails in the club's Massachusetts Room, where the walls are adorned with plaques bearing the names of Harvard men of Massachusetts who have held government office — the names of senators and representatives and governors and judges stenciled in black, those of United States presidents in ubiquitous Harvard crimson.

For many guests, including the evening's featured speaker, Dean of the Faculty of Arts and Sciences Henry Rosovsky, parking before dinner had been a problem. Rosovsky, who several years before had forever endeared himself to Harvard alumni by turning down the presidency of Yale, was finishing his final year as dean. Responsible for a major revision in Harvard's undergraduate curriculum (the change to the Core Curriculum), he was also a familiar figure on the alumni circuit, having made countless speeches before such gatherings. So he could be excused if he began his remarks with the report that he had almost been turned away tonight because parking space was at a premium. Earlier, a club official in black tie had confided to one alumnus, "The members get upset when there isn't room in the lot for them." Then the alumnus had ascended the staircase to the Massachusetts Room, where he signed his temporary club number for a glass of ginger ale, for which he was later billed 79 cents.

Now, the enormously popular Rosovsky was making light of his work by telling jokes about his deanship. He framed his remarks in the form of "thoughts for my successor"; noting that "a university is an unusual mixture of generations," he advised the next dean "to develop a profound sympathy for all Democratic politicians." Throwing a farewell bouquet to alumni ("I will miss you most"), Rosovsky received a standing ovation, which was followed by the singing of "Fair Harvard."

Two scholarship students had preceded Rosovsky to the podium, and one of them, a member of the football team, had introduced his father, who was seated at a nearby table. Since a major goal of the Harvard Campaign was funds for financial aid, and since most alumni at the dinner were contributors to the campaign, this moment raised an awkward question: were the assembled clapping for the student, whose Harvard attendance they were partially supporting, or were they, in a sense, clapping for their own generosity of pocketbook?

Whatever the answer, the alumni maintained a uniformly respectful attention during the student's speech. Most of the men were in black tie, the women in long gowns, and they listened intently as the student sang for his supper, praising Harvard for opening new worlds to him, or new doors — the noun was lost in the clatter of a coffee cup striking saucer across the enormous room, with its wood paneling, vaulted ceiling, balcony with pipe organ, and three chandeliers. Officials and guests, seated on the stage at a long table behind the podium, wore red boutonnieres; their number included a representative of the clergy, who had invoked divine blessing on the occasion. President Bok was not present, though his portrait presided over the proceedings.

Few of the guests lingered when the program came to a close. There was a gentle push to the door, where a long line quickly formed by the coat check. An elderly gentleman in a three-piece suit sat in a leather-upholstered chair, reading *The Wall Street Journal* and smoking a small cigar. Around a corner in the lobby, copies of the latest issue of the club bulletin were available, free of charge. The front-page story invited club members "to take in the excitement and tradition" of the Boston Marathon at the club.

A Boston alumnus who had raised money for Harvard in the Boston area on the occasion of his class's twenty-fifth reunion thought the evening was a success, but he had unkind words for Harvard's professional fund raisers. "The development office didn't help us at all when we were soliciting gifts," he complained. "We did all the work." It had apparently not occurred to him that what he said and the simple fact of his presence at another Harvard function contradicted his conclusion that "development people weren't up to the corporate level" in their ability as executives. "Maybe the reason they don't talk much about what they do is because they have *nothing* to hide," he laughed. "Anyway, Harvard sells itself." Indeed it does, in more ways than he gave it credit for.

Another Harvard dinner. This one was held in the Eliot House dining room one October evening for the combined directors of the Harvard Alumni Association and presidents of Harvard clubs from around the country. The room, with its three chandeliers, ornate wood paneling, and eight high Palladian windows, was filled. People sat at the same tables as do the students, who ate elsewhere that night. The speakers began almost two hours after the scheduled start of the dinner. Alan Heimert, master of Eliot House, referred humorously to the rehabilitation of the Harvard Houses through "ill-gotten gains." Heimert, who is also a professor of American literature, drew mild laughter over this swipe, but his point was indicative of a vague unease over Harvard's money that only occasionally surfaces in such circles. Scholarship checks from three clubs were presented by their presidents to Derek Bok on behalf of Harvard. One representative said, "We came prepared to give you twenty-five thousand dollars, but Dr. ———— said, 'Let's add five thousand.'" There was polite applause.

"Thank you," said Bok.

Harvard's House system, instituted in the 1930s by President Lowell and modeled on the college system at Oxford and Cambridge, was the theme of the weekend program to follow. "Each House now has assigned to it a part of Cambridge," Bok said, speaking of student work in the community. The idea is "to get students in the habit of helping those less fortunate than themselves." The assumption that all Harvard students are fortunate — because they attend Harvard — was implicit. There were few anecdotes and little humor; the speech concluded the program, and Bok immediately ducked out through the nearest door.

The schedule for the rest of the weekend included a meeting of the alumni awards committee, the communications committee, the graduate school relations committee, and several others. Regional directors and club officers shared breakfast at Quincy House on Saturday morning, and there were fourteen items on the agenda for the business meeting of the association. One couple from the Midwest, a lawyer and his wife, said they "come every year." Each guest received upon registration a folder bulging with news about the association and Harvard. Transportation to and from Cambridge was paid for by each alumna or alumnus, as was her or his room, but there was no charge for meals. In some cases, alumni coming to Cambridge for such Harvard business submit a bill for their expenses to Harvard, and the university reimburses them. They then give this money back to Harvard as a tax-deductible contribution. For many of them, and for Harvard, this is small change.

So, too, is the money Harvard spends on more expensive alumni association activities. The budget for a Harvard twenty-fifth reunion is over $700,000, about half of which is subsidized by the university. The rental fee for the use of the Essex County Club is about $10,000; the Pops concert costs about $30,000, the buses cost over that amount. One recent twenty-fifth reunion class spent $11,575.38 for liquor, beer, and wine, and almost $1500 for ice. That class's report cost over $72,000 to produce, of which about $17,000 was covered by voluntary contributions.

Balloons for an event in Eliot House ran almost $400. All this may seem like a lot of money for just a big party, but consider the return on Harvard's investment: better than $10 for every dollar it spends, if you look at it in gross terms of class gift to reunion expense.

That simplistic ratio begs many questions, including how much Harvard would receive if there were no alumni association at all. No loyal alumnus wonders about *that* at a time when the association is growing; recent additions to the fare include short noncredit courses offered at "Alumni Colleges." Working in a historic clapboard building in Harvard Yard (once, briefly, the residence of George Washington as commander-in-chief of the Continental Army) David Aloian is too comfortably ensconced to wonder. Aloian's Harvard is "enormously collegial, highly consultive." It is also orderly, safe, and finally devoid of an appeal to the imagination. It is the Harvard that sends out to alumni a request for brief biographical data for the 1986 *Harvard Alumni Directory* and then invites them to enjoy a prepublication price for the tome of $70.

"As a further bonus for ordering now," concludes a letter over the signature of Charles L. Smith Jr. '50, M.B.A. '55, and at the time president of the alumni association, "you will also receive *Glimpses of the Harvard Past*. This fond look back is likely to become an important piece of memorabilia by itself." A three-color glossy brochure is enclosed with Smith's letter. The brochure is a highbrow version of the flyers for VCRs and personalized doormats sent in the mail with gasoline credit card bills. The back of the brochure trumpets the directory as "The indispensable link to the Harvard community." Inside the brochure, alumni learn that four of Harvard's most distinguished historians, including the same Donald Fleming who so loved to poke fun at the Timothy Learys of Harvard, have contributed essays to *Glimpses*. Harvard — which in other fund-raising publications reminds its alumni that this is where Franklin D. Roosevelt went to school, and Helen Keller, and T. S. Eliot — Harvard here is an advertising medium, shamelessly selling itself.

For its printed appeals to alumni, the Harvard Campaign adopted a crimson-and-white logo that showed French's statue of John Harvard in silhouette. John Harvard, a poor English minister who died in 1638, left his library and half his estate to the college that had been established in 1636. He was the college's first benefactor. French's statue, completed for Harvard's 250th anniversay in 1886, is an idealization.

Raising a chalice on the cover of the final issue of the campaign's newsletter, a caricature of the statue, his youthful face smiling, leans forward in a stone chair, the angle of his knees thrust forward so he looks as though he might stand up after making his toast to all the campaign contributors. Nearly three and a half centuries after his death, John Harvard had become a marketing logo.

Considerable Sums

"Now he would prowl the stacks of the library at night, pulling books out of a thousand shelves and reading them like a madman. The thought of these vast stacks of books would drive him mad: the more he read, the less he seemed to know — the greater the number of books he read, the greater the immense uncountable number of those which he could never read would seem to be. Within a period of ten years he read at least 20,000 volumes — deliberately the number is set low — and opened the pages and looked through many times that number."

Thomas Wolfe was never accused of understatement. Before he wrote the novels that told the story of his own life through his fictional alter ego, Eugene Gant — it is Gant's discovery of Widener Library that is described above — Wolfe was a graduate student at Harvard from 1920 until 1923. No one knows exactly how many books he read while he was there, though later generations of Harvard students, in advertisements for a speed-reading course, were told that Wolfe tried to read everything in Widener, which houses the largest collection in Harvard's system of over one hundred libraries. Wolfe described Gant's roamings in the stacks of Widener as "this fury which drove him."

Dead at the age of thirty-eight, Wolfe would have been eighty-four as the Harvard Campaign neared its end. Though he was never an undergraduate, his later fame would have qualified him for a folder in the office of the campaign staff, where the wealth of a Harvard alumnus can often be guessed by the thickness of his file. From the moment a student leaves the college, the University Development Office may start saving newspaper clippings about him, references to him in corporate reports and club bulletins, copies of any letters he may be vain enough to write to the alumni affairs office — any fact is fit, even, indeed especially, tidbits that a campaign worker or classmate may pick up in his social and professional rounds. "Thomas Wolfe likes to read," a memorandum for the record might have said. And then, clipped to a scathing review of *Look Homeward, Angel* from the Asheville, North Carolina, newspaper, there could have been a notation penned by an area major gifts committee member, who sent in the clip: "Tough prospect. Notorious in these parts. Drinks a lot (this is confidential). Thinks he's a genius. Family was poor, father used to sculpt statues for cemeteries, mother ran a boarding house and it's one place where we're not having our Harvard Club dinner! Very opinionated, says you can't go home again."

Eventually, a summary of Wolfe's folder would have found its way into the hands of a campaign solicitor, with a staff rating of old Tom's giving potential (A, $100,000 or more; BB, $50,000 to $100,000; down to D, $5000 to $10,000). Such ratings, based in part on guesses made by alumni at a series of dinners and luncheons hosted around the country by Harvard before the campaign began, were later refined as the campaign staff sought, too, to predict the prospect's special concerns. Harvard had to learn of its alumni, campaign national co-chairman Robert Stone told a *Harper's* reporter, "not only how much they're worth, but also where their real interest in the college might lie. If there is some special identity they have had with the college — in nominal gifts they have made to the Department of Astronomy, or to science, or to athletics, or to something else — we focus on that." Certainly, Thomas Wolfe would have been told of the plans to spend $3 million of campaign money for a renovation of Widener Library; and perhaps a thoughtful campaign assistant, knowing of Wolfe's interest in literature, might have enclosed in a letter to Wolfe a copy of "Alphabets," written for Harvard's 1984 Phi Beta Kappa exercises by Seamus Heaney, the Irish poet who holds one of the university's most prestigious chairs, Boylston Professor of Rhetoric and Oratory.

Donor research represents the most sensitive subject that can be broached with a Harvard fund raiser. Even the esteemed Dean Rosovksy, who made many campaign calls with Derek Bok, went on the defensive when asked about it. "The research is not scheming," he said, almost apologetically. "I'm a donor, too. There may be exceptions, but Harvard's graduates are pretty well known. I don't know how the research is done. I didn't do it. It was pretty accurate. If alumni were to look at the research reports, they would not be surprised. But I can understand why the campaign staff is skittish about this. It would give an individual the sense that someone was prowling through their private affairs."

One Harvard alumnus harshly referred to the practice as "a criminal invasion of privacy." Short, pithy remarks prepared by the campaign staff for the use of Rosovsky or Bok before a call, campaign *summaries* provided the men with basic, necessary information about a prospective donor. These censored summaries were based on campaign *briefings,* which might contain all manner of private information, including much that an alumnus himself had told Harvard. Some sense of the depth of this material may be gleaned from the fact that the person responsible for keeping track of it was required to have a master's degree in library science or the equivalent.

Basic briefing information might contain a potential donor's employment history, a list of his directorships and trusteeships, a history of his past giving to Harvard, and a summary of his Harvard activities as an undergraduate and alumnus. Any family connection to Harvard would also be included — relatives who had gone to Harvard or taught there or, most important, had given to Harvard. The donor's outside interests would be summarized, with particular mention of his other philanthropic concerns. Finally, Harvard would estimate the donor's net worth by calculating his estimated resources and liabilities. This was the trickiest part of a briefing, for the information on which it was based was the hardest to come by. Corporate annual reports, including a company's so-called 10-K filings with the Securities and Exchange Commission — in which compensation of a company's highest-salaried executives is given — were especially helpful here, but so was the casual remark by a donor's friend or the publicity attendant with the activities of a donor in the sports or entertainment fields.

Fund raisers often have private fun with the material they have gathered. A group of development officers may spend an idle hour estimating which of their wealthiest elderly prospects is a good bet to die in a given year. That way a campaign staff can guess what the chances are for a big bequest. Nor is such discussion simply guesswork. Donors frequently tell Harvard in advance if the university is listed in their wills. The campaign catch was that these amounts could not be credited in advance. The donor had to be dead for such a gift to count.

Dispiriting donor research takes a toll on many development staff members, who spend long hours photocopying, collating, and filing their findings. Their superiors justify the practice as a necessity, and they form elaborate strategies to coordinate the courting of a donor based on the information the research staff has gleaned. These plans, with their cross-referenced columns of solicitors, steps, notes, and dates, look silly in the aggregate, as though fund raising were an elaborate handicapping scheme. Such energy expended, such time invested, often for naught.

Derek Bok can get very angry when someone asks him about

donor research. He has every reason to. The practice is contrary
to the values on which Harvard's community of scholars is based.
Bok retreats to euphemisms. To reveal a "confidence" made in
the gift-giving process, he says, would be "the breaking of a human trust." The truth is that he is too busy to know all that is
going on in the development office, where requests to observe
donor research files are flatly turned down.

David Aloian's alumni association ebullience was mild compared
to that of the national co-chairman of the Harvard Campaign,
Robert G. Stone Jr., also a member of the Harvard Corporation.
Speaking on Commencement Day in 1984 to the afternoon audience assembled for the annual meeting of the Harvard Alumni
Association, Stone announced various reunion class giving totals
and made a short, passionate appeal for a successful campaign.
Stone was a crusader for the campaign cause, and he preached
the Harvard gospel as if it were both a mission and an entitle-
ment. He was a perfect volunteer fund raiser, and he knew it:
  "We are going to need help from each and every one of you —
it's not going to be easy to get to our goal. Reaching our goal on
schedule will call for a very substantial effort, and it will require
a good deal more of the kind of generosity and commitment that
I have been so proud to salute each year since we began in 1979.
  "As we head into the final leg of this capital drive, I would ask
you to bear in mind what reaching the $350 million goal will
mean — not only for Harvard's students and faculty, but for those
institutions of higher education all across the country which look
to Harvard to set the pace. The extent of our success will send a
message far beyond this wonderful and familiar Yard.
  "What we manage to do between now and the end of the campaign will have an impact on learning and scholarship that will
reach throughout the world and will last well into the next century. I ask all Harvard's alumni and friends to think about that
larger context and to respond accordingly."
  Once, back from Nassau, Bob Stone looked around at the pho-

tographs of ships (he had recently stepped down as chairman of West India Shipping Company, Inc.) and sailboats (he was commodore of the New York Yacht Club) decorating the walls of his Park Avenue office, and said apropos of his work for Harvard, "You reach a stage in life when you've done most of what you want to do. You've run companies." A brief pause. Then, "It's important for our society to turn out citizens who will be leaders in the country." And, "You need proper teachers, a proper environment." And, "Look at Harvard's influence in history."

A Harvard class agent "for years and years," Stone also served on different Harvard committees. Succeeding Albert Nickerson on the Harvard Corporation, at the invitation of Derek Bok and then–senior fellow Francis "Hooks" Burr, who personally called on him, he had little idea of the "homework" it would involve. His father, brother, and six children all went to Harvard, which perhaps explained his paternalism.

"I started a scholarship fund in Dad's name. For middle-class families, all-around kids. Harvard sends me a list in December of the kids who are participating. What fun I get out of this." The curtains are closed. Stone is soft-spoken. He is quite tall, his face tanned, his hair neatly combed. His white shirt has bold blue stripes the color of the water in one of the photographs. He is smoking a cigar. It's quiet up here on the twenty-seventh floor of the building. Stone has been in Australia, he mentions, in preparation for the 1987 challenge for the America's Cup. He plays golf; he's a member of the Augusta National Club in Georgia, where the Masters is held every April. "Golf in the winter, sailing in the summer."

Stone's name and that of his father are listed in the *Fund and Gift Supplement to the Financial Report,* published by Harvard each December. Not quite one and a half inches thick, the supplement lists every endowment fund by name and department, and gifts for current use by department and purpose. On page D-84 of the 1983–84 volume, under the general heading "Endowment Funds / Faculty of Arts and Sciences / Beneficiary and

Loan," there is a listing for "Robert G. Stone Flexible Financial Aid Fund (1979)":

- Principal, July 1, 1983 – $1,102,321.81
- Gifts and Other Changes – $24,413.95 (transfer from stabilization reserve)/$239,921.24 (gifts for capital)
- Principal, June 30, 1984 – $1,366,657.00
- Participating units [in the endowment], June 30, 1984 – 9,540.6294
- Unexpended Income, July 1, 1983 – $1.25
- Investment Income – $85,848.46
- Other Receipts and Transfers – none
- Account Income Availed of – $85,848.00
- Unexpended Income, June 30, 1984 – $1.71

Elsewhere in the supplement is a line for another, recent gift of nearly $51,000 made by Stone.

"If the cost of [attending] Harvard became so high that certain students couldn't go," Bob Stone had said, "that would be disastrous. The mix of students makes Harvard the exciting place it is. I feel so strongly about that I would quit — if Harvard couldn't admit certain students because of money."

The Harvard Corporation, according to one of its members, looked not for a person who would define a role, but for one who would fill a role that had already been set. That was how Robert Stone became a fellow before the Harvard Campaign was announced. Harvard needed a New York businessman who could head the drive, and it found a superb one in Stone.

"The campaign staff was sneaky," Stone said. "They'd get my schedule from my secretary, Mrs. Adams. I paced myself, saw a certain number of prospects each week. I had a nice relationship with the staff. They'd come down and see me every two weeks and quiz me: how am I doing, whom should I see? If such people had been a pain in the ass, I wouldn't have done it.

"My hobby, if you will, is venture capital and leveraged buyouts. When I was first on the Corporation, we'd be approving, say, a ten-thousand-dollar budget item, and spend little time on major investments. I said, 'This is cuckoo.'

"It's fun to give. But fund raising distorts your view of some people."

Stone's fellow campaign donor and colleague on the Harvard Corporation, Andrew Heiskell, set up a charitable lead trust to benefit the university. "It pays Harvard a hundred and twenty-five thousand dollars a year, I think," Heiskell said. The gift was the second he'd made to the campaign, the first coming after he'd asked Roy Larsen to give $5 million. "I told Roy, 'If you give that, I'll give five hundred thousand,' which was a considerable sum to me then," Heiskell recalls. Later, he also gave Harvard his Connecticut home, which he believes is worth $1.5 million, and which Harvard will receive — and presumably sell — after Heiskell and his wife have died.

"Roy Larsen," Andrew Heiskell said, "was like a second father to me. We were about a generation apart. I followed in his footsteps in a sense." Larsen, like Heiskell, had been a president of Harvard's overseers, but he hadn't graduated to the Corporation. Before Heiskell approached Larsen for a campaign gift, Larsen had already made a substantial gift several years before to Harvard's Graduate School of Education, which named a major new classroom and office building after Larsen.

Heiskell said he "felt badly" after Larsen made his campaign gift, because Larsen died shortly thereafter. "The stock market was down," Heiskell said, "and I was worried about his family."

Much of Heiskell's campaign time had been spent on what he called "the corporate thing" — raising money from corporations. He hadn't enjoyed that, he said. "You can't go to a company out of the blue and say it ought to put up five hundred thousand dollars for Harvard." Part of the reason for his purported difficulty was personal; Heiskell raised money for other groups, too. "Sometimes I go into a guy's office and forget what organization I'm raising money for. Harvard is not an easy sell. There's too much competition now for money, competing claims." Total corporate gifts to the campaign were more than $11 million. That was little more than half the amount given by foundations, and a fraction of the funds raised from alumni.

Six weeks after the campaign finally ended, its newsletter published interviews with the three national co-chairmen, including Robert Stone, who confessed that little money had been raised in the summer of 1983 because he was busy with the America's Cup races. The campaign had almost died then because one of its volunteer chiefs was overseeing sailboat races in Newport, Rhode Island.

Most private colleges and universities are forthright in their appeals for certain kinds of gifts, though these requests usually reveal more about the intended giver than the receiver. Thus, there appeared in an issue of the *Brown Alumni Monthly* the following advertisement, headed "Preserve Your Assets," which assumed a keen interest in pecuniary matters on the part of its readers:

> The harvest has been bountiful, but now you're faced with the prospect of having the fruits of your labor gobbled up by estate tax. Don't be left in such a pickle!
>
> You can preserve your assets for your children or grandchildren, and, at the same time, make a gift to Brown through a charitable lead trust.
>
> Brown will reap the benefits of the interest income during the term of the trust. Then, at the expiration of the trust, the principal will be passed on to the designated recipient. Those assets will have been removed from your estate and will not be subject to an estate tax at a later time.

Advertisements in *Harvard Magazine* for the Harvard Campaign, which appeared regularly throughout the duration of the campaign, were less direct in their appeal or carried copy of a different tone. One such ad, which featured a four-color photograph of a rower on the Charles River, "challenged" the reader "to do your best for Harvard," because "Harvard challenged you to do your best." Another, entitled "Making a Difference," consisted of a four-paragraph essay by Henry Rosovsky. All such ads carried a thirty-five-word apologia, printed in italics at the bottom of the page, to allay any fears among readers that the publication of the ads compromised the editorial independence of the magazine; instead, the disclaimer, by speaking in the most tortured of institutional prose about the "donation" of the page by the magazine to the campaign, only raised questions where there may have been none.

When the magazine originally announced the Harvard Campaign, there had been a commissioned article by an alumnus from the Class of 1952, Lansing Lamont, called "The College Restored." Also included in that issue was an eight-page descriptive supplement about the campaign written by editor John Bethell. The supplement was, in a sense, the magazine's response to requests by Thomas Reardon, director of the campaign and of the University Development Office, and Fred L. Glimp, vice president for alumni affairs and development, for campaign publicity, says Bethell — "but not in the form they requested." What Reardon and Glimp had in mind, recalls Bethell, was a package put together by some Harvard administrators with a direct stake in the campaign.

Campaign coverage in the magazine after that was "thin and spotty," says Bethell. This caused something of a problem, but "our publisher got us off the hook": the magazine offered the campaign a free page of advertising in each issue. Bethell's feelings about all this "changed as the campaign became less abstract. Physical changes at Harvard" — resulting from campaign money — "were easier to write about." In any event, "the campaign people were very candid — most realized that an out-and-out cheerleading approach wouldn't work. Our readers are by and large very sophisticated."

Bethell, who graduated from the college in 1954, has edited the magazine since 1966. From its founding in 1898 until 1977, the magazine had a paid circulation, with an occasional free issue. A decision to send the magazine to all alumni without charge was not made, Bethell insists, just because the Harvard Campaign was about to be announced. Circulation gains in the late 1960s had been offset by later circulation losses. In the early 1970s, circulation was going up, "but it was costing us a lot to run a paid circulation," says Bethell. The magazine had always had advertising, so that wasn't a new source for funds. "We did a lot of direct mail to increase our circulation," but never more than about one-third of alumni subscribed. The magazine lost money in 1974–75. There was "a financial crisis, and the university had to step in. Long talks followed, and, obviously, one of the considerations in the administration's mind was the coming of the campaign."

The magazine's audience has great demographics — "better than anybody's," Bethell says. Voluntary donations now account for 60 percent of the magazine's annual budget of more than $1 million. There are about thirty-five thousand donors, versus twenty-two thousand paid subscribers in the early 1970s. Ad revenues pay for about a quarter of the budget; the balance is picked up by the university. "We try to rely on the university as little as possible," Bethell says.

A campaign supplement in the September–October 1984 issue was published at Tom Reardon's request. "We felt more comfortable doing it," explains Bethell. "There were good story angles, human angles.

"The campaign *has* made a real difference. There is pride in the new athletic facilities, in the physical renovation of the Houses — which wasn't even emphasized at the beginning of the campaign. It's like the feeling you get after your house is painted." Bethell mentions other factors, too: the junior professorship program set up by Henry Rosovsky with John Loeb's gift, the largest of the campaign; the boost in faculty salaries. Morale is much higher.

To professional administrators in private higher education, particularly career persons in the symbiotic fields of development, alumni affairs, and public relations, the relevant question is: why isn't there more in-house institutional promotion? Accustomed to reading such journals as *CASE Currents* (published by the Washington, D.C.–based Council for Advancement and Support of Education), such administrators may believe the business of education gets short shrift within their own institutions. Here are a few of the fund-raising titles from a list of CASE publications, as presented in a brochure called "Resources": *The Art of Asking: A Volunteer's Guide to Asking for the Major Gift* ("A useful tool to use in training new and experienced volunteers"); *The Effective Case Statement* ("Covers what to include in a typical case statement, how to organize it, how to adapt the case statement to special audiences, and how to use it as a marketing tool"); *An Introduction to Annuity, Charitable Remainder Trust, and Bequest Programs* ("An updated version of the sellout CASE handbook"); *Trustees in Fund Raising* ("Includes identifying and cultivating prospective board members, relationships between development officers and trustees, and roles of trustees in fund raising and policy making").

In 1983–84, voluntary support of higher education was over $5.5 billion, according to the Council for Financial Aid to Education. This figure represented an increase of 8.5 percent over the previous year, the council reported. Leading the list of institutions with the greatest level of gifts received was Harvard University, which includes not only Harvard College, the primary beneficiary of the Harvard Campaign, but thirteen professional and graduate schools, with a reported total of over $125 million; Stanford University, at nearly $112 million, was in second place.

"One of the more engaging aspects of the American way of life," *The New Yorker* once noted in an editorial, "is the long-standing tradition that persons who have made great fortunes by questionable means subsequently atone — either themselves or through their heirs and successors — for their misdeeds by endowing educational institutions that then use the money to finance denunciations of the very misdeeds that made the philanthropy possible."

While the irony inherent in this view of American philanthropy has achieved a mythic credence in American culture, fund raising in private higher education relies on far more than the ancestral guilt of the giver for its success. In fact, today's donor is often a successful, sophisticated individual whose money was just made in a stock market coup or a real estate deal. Before this person makes a gift to the institution of his or her choice, that institution must make a very good case.

The real selling of the institution during the Harvard Campaign took place in small encounters, often one-on-one, involving a Harvard official or volunteer, or both, and the prospect. But long before such a meeting could take place, Harvard had to have presold itself in a process starting when the "prospect" was an undergraduate. Without that base, very few major solicitations were successful. A simple walk around the Harvard campus, which an undergraduate in four years makes more than a thousand times, plants in the future alumnus's mind a subliminal lesson about giving: almost all of Harvard's buildings are named after a past donor, and the undergraduate comes to know many of these names as well as those of the streets in his hometown. Many of the classes a student attends also provide subtle reminders, for they are often taught by professors who hold endowed chairs — a professor's salary paid for with the earnings of someone's gift. Most of these chairs have names, and as a student learns them he continues his education as a prospective donor.

If, then, the first fostering of the impulse to give to Harvard is matched by later, more direct solicitation, there is a middle period during which the prospect is cultivated, and this may take anywhere from a few years to a lifetime. Such activities as those sponsored by the Harvard Alumni Association, as well as the publication of *Harvard Magazine* and the athletic department's annual invitation to subscribe to football tickets, are all a part of this cultivation. The sum of these efforts, combined with further initiatives of the Harvard Campaign, forced Harvard upon the lives of Harvard alumni, some of whom finally made donations just to be rid of the junk mail or the telethon call. Others, of course, thrived on the attention and gave accordingly.

When the Harvard Campaign was announced in 1979, alumni who hadn't already been solicited for an advance gift were told by mail about the largest fund-raising effort in Harvard history. For most alumni, this was the first of many medium-is-the-message announcements and solicitations on the subject they would receive during the next five years, or until they had made their pledge. The instructions on the crimson-colored pledge card read as follows:

> Checks should be made payable to Harvard University and mailed to the Recording Secretary. All gifts to The Harvard Campaign are tax-deductible. Pledges may be paid over a five-year period. All gifts and pledges made during the Campaign period will be credited toward individual and Class Campaign totals. If you plan to donate securities, you should have them placed in a separate account with your agent or broker, with instructions to notify: Office of the Recording Secretary, Harvard University. If you prefer, you may send the unendorsed certificate and, in a separate envelope, a signed stock power directly to the Recording Secretary.

Alumni who responded with a small gift shortly afterward received an acknowledgment, printed by computer on a card illustrated with Harvard's Veritas shield and signed through the printing process with the signature of Schuyler Hollingsworth, recording secretary.

Later, a second acknowledgment arrived. The design for this card varied. By the final year of the campaign, it included a crimson band, and the card had been signed in ink with the name of a classmate, and he — or whoever had done this for him — had added, addressing the alumnus by his first name, "Thanks for your support. Best regards." The printed message said, "Thank you for your recent gift to Harvard, which . . . helps to meet the needs of the College and boosts our class participation."

Harvard men of the past would have cringed at such dry, mechanical prose. Writing to one of his cousins, Henry Lee Higginson, the nineteenth-century founder of the Boston Symphony Orchestra and a major benefactor of his alma mater, Harvard, was direct and florid:

> Nobody knows his duties better than yourself — therefore I presume to admonish you. I want you, as the oldest and richest member of your family and mine, to give the College $100,000, to be used in any way which seems best to suit you.
>
> My reasons are that you, a public-spirited and educated gentleman, owe it to yourself, to your country, and to the Republic. How else are we to save our country if not by education in all ways and on all sides? What can we do so useful to the human race in every aspect? . . .
>
> Democracy has got hold of the world, and *will* rule. Let us see that she does it more wisely and more humanly than the kings and nobles have done! Our chance is *now* — before the country is full and the struggle for bread becomes intense and bitter.
>
> Educate, and save ourselves and our families and our money from mobs.

Major Higginson, whose musicians — or, rather, their successors — play on, and whose munificence, however it may have been prompted, pays bills in Cambridge to this day, was not quoted in any of the official publications of the Harvard Campaign. One of his Harvard gifts, however, was noted in the "Harvard Through the Years" section of the case statement: "1890: Soldiers Field — 31 acres — given by Major Henry Lee Higginson in memory of six Harvard friends who died in the Civil War." Almost one hundred years later, Harvard football teams still play in the stadium that was built in 1903 on that spot, and that bears the same name.

As the Harvard Campaign passed the shaky midpoint of its fourth year in July 1983, the Harvard Management Company, which handles the university's portfolio, had just completed its best twelve months, reporting a total return on the general investment pool of 42 percent. Rather than celebrate investment success in Boston, however, Harvard was concerned about fund-raising stagnation in Cambridge.

At campaign headquarters, located on the seventh floor of Holyoke Center, a glass and concrete structure built in the early 1960s, a receptionist sat in a narrow lobby at the end of an air-conditioned hallway. To her left and right, at equally spaced desks, each with a white desk lamp, sat more than a dozen neatly dressed secretaries, all working solemnly. On the wall above a crimson and blue cushioned couch there was a long bulletin board listing by college class the organization of campaign volunteers. Nearby, displayed on another bulletin board, was a selection of campaign publications, and past the secretaries' desks, on the wall at the end of a white corridor, was a photograph of a white steeple, with a figure written under it — $257,434,075 — the amount of money paid or pledged to the campaign as of that date.

Newspaper clippings were pinned to a third bulletin board. Most were from *The Harvard Crimson* and *The Harvard University Gazette,* and they were uniformly filled with good news about the campaign. The atmosphere was very orderly, like that of a bank, but this center of finance inside Harvard resembled most an advertising agency, one where there was just a single account, with billings to a common client called alumni.

Campaign director Thomas M. Reardon, a tall, heavy-set man wearing gray slacks and a blue blazer, worked in a corner office at the farthest end of one of the corridors guarded by the secretaries' desks. A small couch faced a coffee table and another couch in an alcove with a large window overlooking some of the Harvard Houses and the Charles River beyond. Reardon, who rarely smiled as he spoke, compared part of the campaign's workings to those of the CIA or the Pentagon. He paused after making this grave analogy, as though it reflected on the importance of his post.

A 1962 graduate of Holy Cross who served as press secretary to former Massachusetts governor Francis W. Sargent, Reardon, like many of his colleagues, became involved almost accidentally in what is known in higher education as institutional advancement. He refers to himself as "a custodian." Many at Harvard have done such work before him, he said, and many will follow; part of his job was to ensure that nothing he did disturbed that smooth succession. Proprietary about the institution he served and somewhat defensive about the mysterious methods he and his fellow professionals employed to raise money, Reardon was unwittingly candid as he alluded to "the public relations consequences" of anything written about the campaign. Citing concern about "future campaigns and Harvard's special relationship with certain families" — a relationship he likened to that "of a lawyer and his client, a doctor and his patient" — Reardon explained that much of his work was of a delicate, personal nature. Trust was the backbone of the campaign — trust between donors and Harvard, between the many volunteers who made the campaign possible and the individuals who administered it — and confidentiality was a prerequisite of maintaining that trust.

Tom Reardon was in a difficult position, and he knew it. With just a year and half to go, the Harvard Campaign, trumpeted by the university with all the social zeal and verbal flourish of a holy war when it was announced in 1979, was floundering. The initial pace of giving, which had been so high that in the summer of 1982 the original goal had been raised by $100 million from $250 million, had slackened off. Now the campaign had to average over $5 million per month in new gifts and pledges. Where was the money going to come from? That was the question that Reardon and others inside the Harvard administration were asking themselves; failure was unthinkable.

"Inevitably," stated the glossy, slick, sixty-eight-page campaign prospectus, "the history of Harvard is interwoven with the history of the country. And much that is Harvard — its work, its triumphs, its conflicts and changes — has endured to become a part of the common heritage of America." President Bok appealed to campaign donors in that prospectus "to join the generations that have preceded them in renewing Harvard's commitment to provide educational leadership at the highest attainable level." Modesty has never been a virtue at Harvard, where a legend over a gate to Harvard Yard invites those who pass through it to "enter and grow in wisdom."

Before the Harvard Campaign was announced in 1979, $53 million was already in the campaign kitty. Much of this money — called advance gifts — came from a small group of individuals, many of them overseers or members of the Corporation. Throughout the rest of the campaign, the pattern of a few giving a lot continued; nor was this a surprise to Harvard officials, since traditionally in such campaigns approximately 90 percent of the money raised is given by about 10 percent of the donors.

Like a political campaign, whose purpose (often lost in the rhetoric) is to elect a certain candidate to a certain office, a fund-raising campaign has an objective, or, as was the case at Harvard, objectives. This seemingly trite fact of fund-raising strategy, while of no importance to the donor writing a check for ten dollars or a hundred — gifts that amount to so little they are sought by Harvard primarily because they raise the total percentage of donors and, more important, establish a pattern of giving for each alumna or alumnus — this fact means much to the individual giving upwards of a million dollars or more. He or she wants to know what the money's going for. Accordingly, Harvard prepared a table of campaign objectives, almost all of which were to benefit the undergraduate college (see next page).

These figures, which total $250 million, were revised in 1982, when the campaign goal was increased. However, rather than publish a new table of objectives, which might have called into question the methods by which the original figures were arrived at, Harvard simply stated that the bulk of the increase would be added to the objectives for financial aid and faculty salaries.

At the same time that the original table of objectives was made

STUDENTS IN HARVARD COLLEGE		$89,000,000
Reshaping Undergraduate Education		20,000,000
Core Curriculum	$ 2,000,000	
Dean's Fund	5,000,000	
Small-Group Instruction	7,000,000	
Center for Teaching and Learning	2,000,000	
Innovation Fund	1,000,000	
Equipment and Facilities	3,000,000	
Student Financial Aid		41,000,000
Scholarship Endowment	26,000,000	
Endowed Loans and Subsidies	15,000,000	
The House System		12,000,000
Extracurricular Activities		16,000,000
Athletics	10,000,000	
The Arts	3,000,000	
Memorial Church	3,000,000	
THE FACULTY OF ARTS AND SCIENCES		$88,000,000
Faculty Positions		82,000,000
Endowed Professorships	60,000,000	
Endowed Junior Positions	22,000,000	
Career Development Funds		6,000,000
Sciences	3,000,000	
Humanities and Social Sciences	3,000,000	
RESOURCES FOR RESEARCH AND SCHOLARSHIP		$33,000,000
The Harvard Library		13,000,000
Museums		8,000,000
Laboratory Facilities		12,000,000
CURRENT USE BY HARVARD COLLEGE		$20,000,000
PROGRAMS IN PUBLIC POLICY		$20,000,000

public, so, too, was a table of gifts, which dramatically illustrated where, in gross terms, the money was expected to come from:

Gifts in the Range of	Number Needed	For a total of
$15,000,000	1	
10,000,000	2	
5,000,000	4	
3,000,000	8	
2,000,000	14	
1,000,000	25	
	54	$132,000,000
500,000	50	
250,000	80	
100,000	150	
	280	$ 60,000,000
50,000	200	
25,000	500	
10,000	900	
5,000	1,600	
	3,200	$ 39,500,000
Below 5,000	25,000	$ 18,500,000

Every Harvard alumna or alumnus, save those whose addresses Harvard no longer had or whose names had become lost in a computer disk, received some kind of campaign solicitation, ranging from direct mail to a personal visit from President Bok. Many alumni received several solicitations, and a small, select group were courted repeatedly. An Wang, Ph.D. '48, the chairman of Wang Laboratories, endowed four science fellowships with a gift of $1 million. Wang, who had already given Harvard another $2 million, later added a fourth million when the campaign's goal was raised. Robert Stone visited Karim Aga Khan '58 in Sardinia in the fall of 1984, and in early March 1985, Harvard and the Massachusetts Institute of Technology jointly announced a $9 million gift from him, to fund a master's degree program in Islamic architecture. Together, the two institutions would receive $900,000 a year for ten years under the terms of the gift. Six years before, the Aga Khan had donated $11.5 million, again to both schools, for a program to promote Muslim education and design.

After the campaign and its advance gifts were announced, primary attention was focused on major gifts — those of $100,000 or more. Because of the magnitude of these gifts, and because the solicitation period for them was often lengthy, the "leadership phase" of the campaign continued the full five years. However, little more than a year after the campaign had officially started, the staff and volunteers went into what was classified as the "regional phase," and for two years their effort was directed at alumni in seventy-six cities throughout the country. Concomitant with all these phases, campaign giving was also structured so that alumni in major reunion years — "the fives" — were encouraged to boost their class giving totals for those years. A surprising number of alumni were influenced by this nostalgic incentive.

To this bewildering array of phases and categories, an additional, genuine complexity was the variety of ways an alumnus could give. He could make an outright cash gift or a pledge, payable at the end of the year or over time. He could give securities. He could, if he were in an upper tax bracket and ready to make a large contribution, set up a trust to benefit himself and Harvard. And he could make his gift with no strings attached or direct it toward one of the specific campaign goals. For $1,750,000, he could endow a university professorship; $350,000 put his name on an exhibition gallery in a Harvard museum. There were as many options as those presented a horse player at the track, and the number of different solicitation styles was nearly as great as the thousands of volunteers who gave their time to the campaign. No one person asks another for money in exactly the same way, although there are patterns, and Harvard trained its volunteers as precisely as it could. Instructions to telethon volunteers taught callers, who were to complete ten solicitations in two hours, to "open, engage, ask, and close. Take your time. Listen. Don't rush the conversation. Be alert to the large gift."

But volunteer training, planning, and energy were not a substitute for basic information about the major campaign prospects. The worst mistake a development officer or volunteer can make is to ask for too little, and to avoid this error requires much advance knowledge. This donor requires research — of every conceivable kind — and Harvard's most valuable resource in the process of getting information about its alumni is the alumni. When an alumnus writes in his *Twenty-fifth Anniversary Report* that he's enjoying early retirement in Antigua, he is unwittingly inviting campaign curiosity about his financial resources.

Fund raising is not a science, despite the claims its practitioners may make for it. All the financial and biographical information in a development office folder means nothing in the hands of the wrong solicitor. Were that not the case, Tom Reardon wouldn't have been so worried that all his efforts might be for naught; he would only have had to review the rules, apply them, and collect the checks. But Reardon knew that a good fund-raising operation is divided into two parts, research and solicitation; neither works well without the other. At the most fundamental level of a campaign, alumni don't give money — they are asked to. Volunteers who forget this will report with triumph that a donor has just pledged, say, a thousand dollars, only to learn that Harvard was expecting ten thousand. One has to *ask* for the larger gift; it rarely comes unsolicited.

After a Harvard alumnus of rumored or documented means — "a heavy hitter," in the vernacular — was identified, he was usually solicited for a gift to Harvard by another alumnus of comparable wealth. But one call is often not enough; many large gifts require a solicitation strategy employing several alumni and officials from the university, who travel around the country to conduct their business. Such solicitation requires a combination of diplomacy and tenacity, and at Harvard there are few better at it than Reardon's boss, Fred Glimp.

Glimp, Harvard '50, Ph.D. '64, was dean of admissions in the 1960s, and he later became dean of the college; he left Harvard shortly after the student revolt in 1969. Glimp headed the Boston Permanent Charities Fund for nearly a decade, before rejoining the fold in 1978, the year before the Harvard Campaign was announced. A handsome, affable man at ease with himself, Glimp welcomed campaign visitors to his Massachusetts Hall office with the warmth of old friends, even if he had never before met them.

Wearing a pinstripe suit, white button-down shirt, and a quiet red-print tie, Glimp frequently clasped his hands behind his head as he spoke. His short, graying hair was neatly combed, his voice soft. "Of course, Tom [Reardon] knows more about this than I," Glimp said, referring to the campaign. He was smiling; sometimes, before continuing, he made his brow furrow, but he never lost the smile. Glimp spoke modestly about his career, said one of the things he liked most about being back at Harvard was the chance to meet alumni he'd admitted as freshmen and to find out what they were now doing. Class reunions, he said, were "grand occasions!" The exclamation mark was one of many. At an institution where most people practiced understatement, Fred Glimp loved superlatives.

Portraits of Fred Glimp as a Harvard fund raiser filled the pages of campaign publications. They always showed a smiling Glimp chatting with alumni. "Mr. Charles F. Kaye who, with his wife, Mary, is chairing the Harvard-Radcliffe Parents Fund this year, meets with Vice President for Alumni Affairs and Development Fred L. Glimp '50," read the caption accompanying a posed shot of Glimp and Kaye chatting. The multiple purpose of this publicity had nothing to do with rewarding Glimp for his tireless travels. Rather, it placed repeated visual images of Glimp before alumni so they would eventually think of *him* when they thought of the campaign. They would *expect* a call from him.

And when he called, they would already know him; they had seen him visiting with their friends. It was Glimp who went on the road for the campaign, while Tom Reardon stayed home and minded the store. You couldn't spend any time with this man, reminiscing about Harvard or discussing the Olympics or telling jokes, without wanting to give money — to Glimp. The checks, of course, were made out to Harvard, but it was Glimp who talked with alumni, who cared about their children and their work, who could laugh about growing old. Glimp was one of them.

Entering Massachusetts Hall, next to Johnston Gate, through which he had walked so many times, Fred Glimp felt the breeze on his back disappear as the door closed behind him; without breaking the bounce to his step, he greeted the receptionist at her word processor with a brief, cheerful "Morning, Priscilla," and walked upstairs to his office. Late for work (it was almost ten o'clock) Glimp put down his briefcase, glanced at some letters on his desk, and lit a Winston. Despite public pronouncements to the contrary, the successful completion of the Harvard Campaign was very much in doubt, and Glimp was determined to make each day, each call count.

Glimp was running behind schedule. Just back from Alaska, he had correspondence to read and answer, three meetings to attend — one after the other, with no breaks in between — and his secretary was away. He was taking no telephone calls. It would be after seven before he arrived in Belmont, the Boston suburb where he still lived until his posh new condominium near the John F. Kennedy School of Government was ready to be occupied.

Despite the demands on his time, Glimp remained relaxed and convivial. The plane trip home had been a long one, but he wasn't bothered by jet lag. And, like the professional traveler he was, he'd focused exclusively on the business reasons that had necessitated his being in the forty-ninth state. Asked his impressions of the place, he had to think twice before answering,

"It was great!" Sightseeing hadn't been on his agenda. Money had.

Glimp's faith had been severely tested in 1969 and during the aftermath of the student strike, and getting away from Harvard for a while, as he had been planning to do for some time before the strike, was just what he had needed. He hadn't expected to return, but when he did he found that the wounds — his wounds, his damaged pride in the institution — had healed. He'd been through what seemed the worst any college administrator could endure — being ordered from his office, watching as students whom he'd admitted to Harvard forcibly evicted his colleagues, listening as other students who were gathered outside in the yard shouted, "Strike! Strike! Strike!" — and he'd survived. So had Harvard. There was no point in looking back; when someone spoke with him about what had happened, he artfully changed the subject. Now, so close to meeting its revised goal, the campaign was at a do-or-die stage; but this, too, Glimp understood, and he wasn't worried. Campaigns always finished in a kind of burst, and he saw no reason that wouldn't be the case at Harvard in the second half of 1984. In fact, so certain was he that Harvard would prevail, he'd recently been daydreaming about what he should say when the inevitable questions were asked at the end of the year about who was responsible for the success.

The details of that success he kept to himself. "Never discount the importance of luck in institutions," he'd say. But Fred Glimp didn't need to explain his success. It was there, an open secret every time he met alumni. Other fund raisers were ambassadors or salesmen or businessmen; to Harvard's alumni, Fred was their friend.

The March–April 1984 issue of *Harvard Magazine* reported that, "To stimulate giving, the Campaign's executive committee announced on January 24 [1984] the formation of a $25-million challenge fund, composed entirely of increased pledges by the 27 members of the committee and three others.

"Every new or increased capital gift," the article continued, "and all contributions to the reactivated Harvard College Fund during 1984 will be matched on the basis of one dollar for every two donated. . . . If the fund is fully earned, the Campaign will meet or exceed its $350-million goal by December 31, 1984."

With help from the Challenge Fund, and by some literal stroke of good fortune or through an accountant's feat of legerdemain, the Harvard Campaign was able in June of 1984 to announce that it had almost exactly reached the $300 million mark in pledges and gifts. This meant that about $33 million, with a $17 million Challenge Fund match, was needed to reach the goal of $350 million.

Led by a tired-looking but driven Tom Reardon, the campaign staff settled down for the final six-month push. Fresh from his golf lessons and a few days off after reunion, David Dearborn took up his familiar perch, down the hall and around the corner from Reardon, in an office marked "Class Endowment Program." Around another corner, past many more branch offices of the campaign, Joseph G. Carr, director of communications, was busy putting together the latest issue of *The Harvard Campaign Report*. Like his colleagues, Carr was planning no vacation this summer.

Across Massachusetts Avenue in Wadsworth House, David Aloian was sifting through the preliminary figures for reunion week: number of alumni present, number of spouses and children, cost of food, cost of housekeeping, and so on. The final tallies would not be ready until October, but Aloian was buoyant about the success of this year's big week. Looking up from his neatly organized desk, he termed the overall attendance "unbelievable."

Another summer had come to Cambridge, and with it an outward calm to Harvard Yard. Where, the week before, thousands of people had congregated for commencement, now a solitary sunbather spread a blanket on trampled grass. Students had left for summer jobs and travel, professors could spend their time in

Widener Library and their laboratories or on vacation, and certain administrators — those not directly responsible for raising and managing and administering the money that made the continuation of their paradise possible — could catch up or take a break themselves.

John Bethell, editor of *Harvard Magazine,* was checking galley proofs while planning for a trip to the Soviet Union he was going on shortly with the Harvard-Radcliffe Orchestra. "Maybe I'll get a story out of it," he said. "Mostly, I just want to see Russia." Professor William Alfred, who lives in a modest home on a quiet side street behind several of the Harvard Houses, was leaving soon for England, where his latest play was about to receive its première, with Faye Dunaway in the lead. Alfred, who occasionally lectures on the Harvard alumni circuit ("I generally talk about the working theater and conclude with an excerpt from one of my plays; I have no idea why people come to see me"), was one day entertaining a student in his living room, serving him iced tea with mint and talking to the student about his English honors thesis. John Bethell said he "envied anyone who was spending time with Alfred."

Though they were not part of the campaign staff, Bethell and others, such as the long-time director of information in the Harvard University News Office, Deane W. Lord, played an important fund-raising role. Their work, while independent of the empire ruled by Tom Reardon and Fred Glimp, was nevertheless designed to spread the good word. Both would have bridled at the suggestion, but behind the independent, daily decisions they made was the realization that their primary constituents (to use a favorite institutional advancement word) were the same people courted by the Harvard Campaign. No one told them what to do, but that is because it was not necessary. Like all Harvard administrators, they both knew. Only professors have academic freedom.

Energetic, highly vocal, and possessed of a slightly irreverent but deeply felt passion for Harvard, Lord takes charge of a conversation the way a good field marshal oversees a battle. She won't let anything slip by. Hundreds of books and magazines were stored on shelves and stacked on the carpeted floor in what appeared to be random fashion. Copies of *The New Republic* lay near *The Chronicle of Higher Education,* and outside the door there were several dozen leftover media kits for commencement, which contained the text of an address by honorary degree recipient King Juan Carlos I of Spain, and a fifteen-page press release, which had been marked for release at 11 A.M. on Commencement Day. Lord had something to say about each item, and it was quickly clear that she maintained in her head an inventory of all she had read and written about Harvard. And, like John Bethell, she was unafraid of giving what many more timid institutional advancement officers falsely believe is a public relations blunder: opinions.

Lord's recall of writers and their work was exceeded only by her recollection of Harvard alumni she had known. She spoke with affection of David McCord, Harvard's unofficial poet laureate, who lives at the Harvard Club in Boston. It was McCord who in 1936 penned the most famous and most sentimental Harvard lines ever used in the official publications of the college. Still quoted, their diction is very different from the language of contemporary Harvard fund raising:

> "Is that you,
> John Harvard?"
> I said to his statue.
> "Aye — that's me," said John,
> "And after you're gone."

Spurred on by the carefully timed announcement of a $2 million gift from John W. Blodgett Jr. '23 of Grand Rapids, Michigan, the Harvard Campaign now needed just $6 million, with a $3 million Challenge Fund match, to meet its goal. One Harvard official confessed that the Blodgett gift had been known for some time and that, with "one good day in the stock market," the campaign would be over the top.

The weather had been unseasonably warm, and the snow from a December storm had melted. It was cloudy one morning, and by afternoon a cold rain fell. The stores were very crowded, with lines at the Harvard Coop ten to fifteen people deep. In the center of Harvard Square, the old subway kiosk had just been reopened as part of the final stage of reconstruction of the subway line through the square. The trains now went another two stops, and no longer reversed direction in the yards near the Charles River for the return trip to Boston. Students had left for winter vacation, and there was not another meeting of the Harvard Corporation until mid-January. The overseers would not convene again until the first weekend of February. William Bentinck-Smith, former editor of the alumni magazine and former assistant to Nathan Pusey, was completing his revision of Samuel Eliot Morison's *Three Centuries of Harvard*. He'd been commissioned for the job by the president and fellows in anticipation of the 350th anniversary celebration in 1986. Derek Bok was in town; at dusk, when the streetlights around the square were turned on, shoppers and commuters waiting at the bus stop on Massachusetts Avenue by Johnston Gate could see the lights inside his office. A green wreath with red decorations hung on the main door of Massachusetts Hall.

In Cambridge that December, as copies of the 1983–84 *Financial Report to the Board of Overseers of Harvard College* were being distributed, here were the front-page headlines from a pre-vacation issue of *The Harvard Crimson:*

ART's Controversial 'Endgame' Production Opens
After Beckett Law Suit is Resolved

Court Acquits Student Of Assault Charges

Ministers Demand Divestiture From South African Interests

Study Shows AIDS Not A Danger
to Health Workers

President Bok Visits Mather [House], Discusses Crowding,
Class Size

Panel Finds 'Nuclear Winter' Possible

Despite the Mailgrams to campaign volunteers as the year 1984 ended, there was little real celebration when the Harvard Campaign made its goal. The day *The Harvard Crimson* ran the news, there were also page-one stories about an agreement Harvard had reached to repay the federal government several million dollars in overcharged research costs and about another hurdle in the regulatory process that the medical area power plant, MATEP, had passed. The official campaign tally was now $353 million, but year-end gifts were still coming in. Assistant Treasurer Henry Ameral said in early January he was expecting more. Harvard had spent about $21 million, or 6 percent of the total raised, to conduct its campaign. This was much less than the national average for fund-raising campaigns, which is about 9 percent.

The reason for the relatively subdued reaction over the campaign's success was simple: though the campaign was over, the quest for more gifts was not. Long before December 31, 1984, Harvard had been preparing for the resumption of its annual giving program aimed at alumni, called the Harvard College Fund.

Established in 1925, the fund had been dormant during the five years of the campaign, but its continuation afterward was vital to the college's financial health. A new chairman of the fund, Henry G. van der Eb '42, had been selected, and former director of admissions William R. Fitzsimmons '67 had been appointed executive director.

A. Michael Spence, who had succeeded Henry Rosovsky as dean of the Faculty of Arts and Sciences, had addressed a letter to all alumni in October. He appealed to them to make a gift to the fund — a gift that, if it were pledged or received by the end of the calendar year, would also be credited to the campaign and, therefore, be eligible for a Challenge Fund match.

Tom Reardon talked about the impact on charitable giving of proposed changes in tax law during a January regional conference of the Council for Advancement and Support of Education (CASE), held at the pricey new Westin Hotel in downtown Boston. Representatives from as far away as Nova Scotia and Maryland attended the four-day annual event, which was billed as "Advancement by CASE."

A wide range of programs was described in the conference booklet's institutional vernacular. There were "plenary sessions" involving "discussants," a cocktail party called "a study in light libation," professional development seminars on such subjects as "Moving Along In Your Career Path," special fifteen-minute meetings (by appointment) with "mentors" to go over "problem situations" in a format called "mentoring," and a host of other seminars and panel discussions, organized around the participant's advancement area or "track" (alumni administration, communications, and educational fund raising).

Harvard used to cast a cold eye on these affairs, but now it sent several people in addition to Reardon. John Bethell moderated a periodicals seminar on "Writing People Will Read," Deane Lord was a panelist in a session called "The Creative Periodical Team," Richard Boardman, director of special and general gifts, was a panelist looking at the question, "To Be or Not To Be: Or What Do You Do With the Annual Fund When You Are Conducting A Capital Campaign," and David Rosen, associate vice president for news and public relations, who came to his job via experience on MATEP, was part of a panel discussing "Trial by Media." (The description read: "Frequently colleges and schools are being hit with law suits, threats of law suits, or inquiries by government agencies on everything from alleged unfair labor practices, to harassment, to discrimination. Inevitably it will make the news. How to handle media relations during these sensitive situations.")

Reardon spoke on the last day of the conference at a capital campaigns and major gifts seminar, "Making Your Goal." Flush from the successful completion of the Harvard Campaign, Reardon faced an audience of over two dozen colleagues from such schools as Bowdoin College and Amherst College.

"It's difficult to talk about making the goal if you don't start the first day of planning," he said. Reviewing the Harvard Campaign, he cited the formulation of the campaign's packaged prospectus, or case statement, as a way "to forge internal consensus and set deadlines."

He recalled a dinner for a dozen "alumni leaders" and President Bok, which was followed within a year by two more meetings of the same group, who were then each asked to convene meetings of fifteen to twenty other people. After about eighteen months, Reardon explained, "over seven hundred people were involved in the process."

More meetings with alumni had followed, as Harvard weighed "the tolerance of alumni and the [giving] capacity of alumni" before setting a campaign goal "that was not so high it couldn't be achieved." Alumni were asked to rate the giving potential of their classmates and neighbors, "and out of that, through more art than science, we set a goal." By then, two years into the planning, the number of people involved had grown to over four thousand. The number of volunteers would eventually total over five thousand, although only ten of them, Reardon said, "were first rate." The original core group of alumni leaders, supplemented by a few others, would become the campaign's executive committee, whose members included Derek Bok (himself a campaign contributor), John L. Loeb, former president Nathan Pusey, and David Rockefeller '36.

Reardon spoke rapidly, without notes, about the campaign's "keeping an even keel, sort of going upward"; about the use of outside consultants (there were, initially, two); about the way in which revising the goal midway had had a kind of "re-creative" effect, putting those involved in the campaign back through the planning process.

He contrasted the solicitation for major gifts with the series of six-month regional efforts for smaller ones. He cited the importance of the Challenge Fund; without naming him, called Robert Stone "the greatest fund-raising chairman that God put on earth"; and explained how during the campaign "major donors became major solicitors."

Smiling, Reardon turned several of his answers in reply to questions from the audience into extended comments about the organization of the Harvard Campaign. He seemed relaxed, raising his eyebrows before launching into an anecdote about a wealthy Alaskan alumnus "who wanted to have a campaign there, so we had one. We're very flexible." His teeth showed as he smiled, and he frequently began an answer with the word *yes,* stretching it with his deep Boston accent into two and sometimes three syllables.

Explaining to his CASE conference audience why the Harvard Campaign had raised its goal from $250 million to $350 million, Reardon admitted that, in part, Harvard had simply realized it "had the ability to raise more money." But there was another, economic reason, Reardon said. "Clear, objective factors had changed the climate," he continued. "Inflation was up, and financial aid and scientific research grants were down." In addition, the House renovations, which had originally been budgeted at $12 million, were now going to cost about $60 million. "This," Reardon said, "was a little harder to explain to our alumni." Once the work had started, Harvard discovered that the buildings were in poorer repair than had been realized; for example, old wiring was found to be unsafe, and had to be replaced at a huge cost and with nothing, on the surface, to show the donor who footed the bill. You couldn't name new wiring after a donor, and nearly all of the Houses already had been named for benefactors. Consequently, this was hard money to raise.

The Challenge Fund was created when a member of the campaign's executive committee said, according to Reardon, "I'll put up another five million if the rest of the group [together] will put up another twenty million." With a few other individuals, the committee came up with the money.

On the campaign travel circuit, one of the national co-chairmen was "a traveling salesman," Reardon said. Faculty members were involved, "to spread the burden."

It was probably a mistake, Reardon said, to have dropped the annual Harvard College Fund drive during the campaign. Doing so was "a political compromise, not a fund-raising decision." Also, the campaign had adopted a "single-ask" philosophy, in which alumni could request that there be no further campaign solicitation once they had made a gift. There was, Harvard learned, no reason to have done this — very few alumni seemed concerned about being asked more than once — and when the goal was raised the campaign staff had to revise this approach.

Reardon talked about how "tremendously important" it was to screen prospective donors and predict their giving potential, admitted that Harvard had never done very well raising gifts from parents (during the campaign, the annual level of parent giving went from about $70,000 to about $400,000, he said), and finally, after running past the scheduled ninety minutes of his presentation, turned to the most important professional problem then facing everyone in educational fund raising: the predicted decline in charitable giving if certain changes took place in tax laws governing charitable deductions.

One such proposed change, to lower the marginal tax rate, would be a "disincentive" to charitable giving, Reardon said. Of another, to change the deduction allowed for gifts of property that have appreciated in value, Reardon had a single word to describe the impact: "devastating."

In the maze of rules and regulations governing the computation of an individual's federal income tax, several things stand out with respect to charitable giving. A primary concern is a donor's marginal tax rate. For 1984 taxes, due in April of 1985, that rate was 50 percent of adjusted gross income. The effect of an individual's marginal tax rate on his charitable deductions can be summarized very simply. For every dollar that individual gives to charity, the actual cost to him is reduced by an amount equal to his tax rate times each dollar given. What this means is that the federal government is really subsidizing that taxpayer's charitable gifts, and the rate of the subsidy equals the person's tax rate. In fact, and exclusive of any changes in tax policy that may have taken place since the Harvard Campaign ended, charitable contributions such as those made to Harvard often involve many other complicated tax considerations, including estate planning. But in the example given of a dollar donated in 1984 — a dollar, let us say, donated to the Harvard Campaign — the actual cost to the donor of that gift must be reduced by multiplying it by his tax rate. Thus, to an individual in the 50 percent bracket, the real cost of a donated dollar was 50 cents, since the other 50 cents was deducted from his tax liability. In other words, the federal government "gave" half of the gift.

A significant portion of gifts to the Harvard Campaign were of appreciated property, and here, too, the tax laws were critical in figuring the real cost of such gifts. Under IRS regulations still in effect in 1984, gifts of certain property that had realized long-term capital gains could be deducted at their fair market value. Assuming that value was greater than what the donor originally paid for the property, this meant in many cases that the donor's tax deduction was also greater than the amount of the original purchase.

The actual application of these basic rules, within the framework of the overall tax code, and with the addition of infinite variables based on the kind of gift made and the financial circumstances of the donor, are Byzantine in their overall form and beyond complete explication in their result. To put it differently, no two gifts are exactly alike. But the dependence of charitable organizations such as Harvard on the instrument of tax policy as a factor of their own finances can be stated unequivocally. The charitable tax deduction is one of the foundations of Harvard's financial planning. Without it, everything else in the equation would change. Within Harvard, the subject came up all the time. Harvard even published its own book about it, *The Harvard Manual: Tax Aspects of Charitable Giving*. The 1983 edition of that volume, the fifth one put out, was 168 pages long.

Michael T. Boland, Harvard's director of planned giving, stood by the doorway of the Westin Hotel's Adams Room, waiting for Tom Reardon. Boland, who'd participated the day before in a CASE conference seminar entitled "Capital Campaign and Major Gifts: Integrating and Crediting Planned Giving," was on his way back to Cambridge after a morning meeting. He'd stopped to see Reardon without having made any prior plans to do so. The two men saw each other often enough in Holyoke Center, where their offices were two floors apart, but here they could talk privately, without an agenda or the interruption of the phone. They shook hands warmly and departed deep in conversation after Reardon's final remarks, which Boland had heard. "We're looking now at the annual fund, which may produce eleven or twelve million this year," Reardon had said, "but the Faculty of Arts and Sciences may need forty million. It costs about four million to put a research chemist in the lab today."

The subject of tax changes was very much on Boland's mind, for the office he headed depended on the advantageous use of tax law to make deferred giving possible. It was Boland's office that published *The Harvard Manual* and, in concert with investment professionals at the Harvard Management Company, worked with individual donors (to the college or to one of the graduate or professional schools) in the planning and implementation of a deferred gift. "We're sort of a service organization to the development office," Boland said. "We don't have a constituency ourselves." Planned giving, Boland pointed out, was mentioned in all of Harvard's development literature and at fund-raising meetings. That was the usual way in which a donor found out about Boland's office.

Boland came to Harvard in 1976 from the University of Rochester. The Planned Giving Office at Harvard that he took over in 1979 had been started in 1974. Nothing else in fund raising is as complicated, from a technical standpoint — or, until some recent changes in the regulations, as profitable for the donor and Harvard — as a deferred gift. Planned gifts operate on a different threshold from more conventional donations; the minimum gift to start a trust with Harvard as beneficiary is $50,000. "There

are things I know that I can't write down," said Boland, empha-
sizing the confidentiality of the financial and personal information some donors give him.

The Harvard Manual defines a deferred gift as "simply an ir-
revocable gift of a remainder interest (in cash or property) to
Harvard with respect to which the Donor has retained a benefit
for himself or his named beneficiaries for a stated period." Another Harvard publication defines the various kinds of such gifts.
A charitable remainder unitrust "pays the life-income beneficiary
a percentage of the fair market value of the trust assets as reval-
ued annually," while a charitable remainder annuity trust "pays
the beneficiary a fixed amount each year as determined by the
donor and Harvard. . . . The charitable lead trust is a mirror image of the charitable remainder trust." A pooled income fund " is
similar to a mutual fund. Individual gifts are combined and assigned proportionate interests in a common fund."

Prior to 1983, when the IRS assumed only a 6 percent return
on the assets of a charitable income (lead) trust (that figure rose
to 10 percent in 1983) it was possible for a donor to make a
substantial gift to Harvard *and* make a profit for his heirs with
such a trust, in which Harvard gets the income or "lead interest"
and the remainder goes to a beneficiary or the donor. Even Boland, who insists "there are no free lunches today in deferred
giving," admits that the only liability to the donor in such a situation was the loss of other opportunities to invest the money.
Harvard maintains special computer programs to project the results of such trusts, and it offers counsel to the donor in explaining the intricate options of other deferred gifts, which include
gifts of stocks and bonds, real estate, tangible personal property,
life insurance, intangibles other than stocks and bonds, bargain
sales, and gifts of oil and gas interests.

Ideally, said Boland, eight to ten months pass from the time a
donor inquires about a deferred gift until he makes one. There
may be anywhere from three to five visits between the donor or
his representative and Harvard during that time. "Up front," Bo-

land said, Harvard works out for the donor what the charitable deduction of his contemplated gift may be. It's important, Boland stressed, "to quickly show the donor something real."

The typical donor of such a gift "is very philanthropic. He will have exhausted the amount of deduction he can use and the so-called carryover, and the discussion moves to the estate tax schedule." In that discussion, the role of the Harvard Management Company, Boland added, "is very important. I can't quantify it, but it's essential." When complicated gift situations arose — for example, a certain piece of real estate with business ramifications — Boland called Henry Ameral at the management company.

Ameral, who began working for Harvard in 1960 and described himself as "sort of the person who's done everything," spoke passionately of "so many people, throughout their working lives, making gifts, many alumni year after year doing the best they can, and some of them really straining, because it's not so easy for them to do this every year." He described the "big gifts" as "a good thing to do and good business decisions." Million-dollar gifts may receive most of the publicity, but a $10,000 gift from a donor whose income is $100,000 is "a big thing." Deferred giving "is a nice way to raise money," Ameral said. "It provides for the donor all of the things he really wanted to do.

"Derek often says that's a tough way to raise money. Yeah, it's tough." It was also profitable. "There's a feeling of family," he continued, mentioning the trust and pooled income fund donors with whom he corresponds on a quarterly basis.

With the advent of ever more complicated giving arrangements, the computerization of records and projections, and the prospect of changes in the tax laws that make many of the gifts sensible, Ameral emphasized the personal in his discussion of donors and of his own work. "Every single security gift must reach my desk," bragged Ameral, who officially splits his time between two posts: treasurer of the Harvard Management Company and assistant treasurer of the university.

When a gift is made to Harvard, the recording secretary records it before sending it to Ameral. If the gift is real property, a nominal value is assigned to it — say one dollar — for recording purposes, and this value is not changed until the property has been appraised and converted to cash. If the gift is a security, the date the donor signed the stock power may be recorded as the date of the gift. Or a gift's date may be the date it was mailed. "The best date the donor intended," was the way Ameral put it. This can be important for year-end gifts when the donors compute their taxes, but Harvard will not take a gift clearly made in January and credit it for tax purposes in December.

The campaign, Ameral continued, "opened up" deferred giving at Harvard. It also "produced many strains on the management company," which had to manage the funds from the gift. Ameral credited Harvard's treasurer with having the vision to recognize the importance of deferred gifts as "the best vehicle that a university or charitable organization can offer its well-endowed alumni."

Several times a year, a group called Friends of Harvard Track sends out an appeal for money. This group is one of many at Harvard that raise special funds for specific purposes. One request from the Friends of Harvard Track was for gifts to support an international track competition between Oxford-Cambridge and Harvard-Yale. A Harvard alumnus whose Harvard track career had lasted one week received the regular mailings from the Friends of Harvard Track. This same alumnus received similar mailings from the Harvard University Band, in which he had played one year. He had never given any money to either group, but he still was considered a "friend."

"We resent the day," wrote the late Harvard professor Willard Sperry, "when in the order of nature it becomes our duty to hand over a bigger check than we think we can at the moment afford, in response to the high-powered salesmanship of some classmate, who is insistent that 'good old '94' shall not fall behind the gift of '93 and shall set the bar a bit higher for '95. It is, however, the method that irks us, not the cause."

In its public discussion of the campaign, Harvard preferred to stick to campaign ends, not means. "The needs that must be addressed by this drive are urgent and fundamental," a campaign publication proclaimed, "not only for Harvard, but for all colleges and universities. A successful Harvard Campaign for $350 million will have a direct and vitalizing effect on American higher education, and the future leadership and productivity of our entire nation."

"To me, of course," Henry Rosovsky told a New York City alumni audience in 1980, "our needs are clear and obvious, but when I travel throughout the country — begging bowl in hand — I frequently encounter a question asked openly or only by implication. Does Harvard *really* need more money? Or are we, the most heavily endowed university in the country, crying poor?" Employing statistics about the rising cost of fuel to heat Harvard's buildings, the declining level of faculty salaries, and other financial matters, Dean Rosovsky argued the case for the campaign in terms that were as unassailable as they were, to the outsider, uninspiring.

For Rosovsky, the campaign signified another milestone in an odyssey that began with his birth in the Free City of Danzig in 1927. He passed his childhood in Gdansk, Poland, and attended college in the United States, graduating in 1949 from William and Mary (the second-oldest American college). A Harvard master's degree and Ph.D. followed, and he taught at Berkeley for six years before returning to Cambridge in 1965. Chairman of Harvard's economics department from 1969 until 1972, he was chosen by Derek Bok as dean of the Faculty of Arts and Sciences in 1973. Soon he found himself asking Harvard alumni for campaign gifts, and he proved very adept at it. He and Bok were an unlikely pair, the president wishing he were doing something else and the dean having the time of his life.

"I met many wealthy people," the pipe-smoking Rosovsky said one day. "I learned they have to be careful. They have elaborate security devices in their homes." He was always received courteously, he said. "There was pride that the dean of the faculty was calling on them." The feeling was mutual.

Rosovsky, who boasted there were no expense accounts at Harvard (the "exact way to see that expenses are minimized"), who said of Harvard's campus, "There is a lot of beauty here," who asked, "When did the Harvard mystique really soar?" and answered, "Since the Depression," warned that the phone was apt to ring. No calls came for fifty minutes; then there were several. A few months had passed since Rosovsky, at the age of fifty-seven, had relinquished his dean's post, and he was in a talkative, reflective mood.

"All university administrators have to say they don't like what they're doing, because the essence of our occupation is teaching and research. And that's exactly what we can't do as administrators. It's an odd thing. Derek and I together did the bulk of the out-of-town campaign work. There were, for the campaign, many forms of activity — much public speaking, many small dinners, and a great deal of calls to the people who require personal solicitation. This often included return trips. It was not always easy. Many find it hard to ask for the gift. Virtually everyone gives something, but to accomplish something with their gift individuals must stretch. Harvard is not the only thing in people's lives. For some people, giving is an emotional thing. Others have very definite ideas for the gift, and they're not always the administration's. Then creativity of all kinds comes in. These are not necessarily bad donations — just those you don't need or want.

"This Harvard Campaign was different. On the one hand, what's the big deal? But this one was to raise unrestricted funds, and that's the most difficult to raise. You have to convince the donors that it will make a difference to do this. Harvard has also been honest in its accounting, versus a public relations exercise.

"In eleven years as dean, I must have talked to hundreds and hundreds of individuals. Some of the calls I made were with Bok, some alone. I was thoroughly briefed by the campaign staff; a staff member even came to the calls. It was necessary to make these calls in person. People like to be told. They don't want to read about it. I would sometimes suggest a gift, and sometimes found I was far off.

"The junior professorships endowed with John Loeb's gift are close to my heart. One day I was in Loeb's apartment in New York City. There was a gorgeous collection of paintings. 'You know, Henry,' Loeb said, 'I just had them appraised. Maybe I should give them to Harvard.' I blanched. 'But I guess that wouldn't help you very much.'

"The campaign was also an opportunity for people to vent their dissatisfaction over such things as an alumnus's displeasure that his son was turned down for admission. Also, since we live in an extremely competitive world, this was a chance for every Harvard man and woman to test. 'Why are there all those liberals in the economics department?' You really have to listen and really have to answer. I got angry once or twice. But the occasion doesn't call for it. I never got a sense of people feeling, 'Why is he running around raising money?'

"Is Harvard good at raising money? You have to take everything in its particular sociological context. For example, Stanford is very successful tapping the new wealth of California. To some extent, Harvard continues to depend on old wealth. But one of the things this campaign did was draw in for the first time some of the new wealth. Self-made people are often very generous. The campaign surfaced a great deal of these people."

The official Harvard Campaign tally in January 1985 had come to $358 million. In the forthcoming issue of *Harvard Magazine* there would be an article about it (*"The largest capital drive ever undertaken for undergraduate education raises $358 million.* Bravo, Harvard Campaign"). Fred Glimp was reported to have "logged between 100,000 and 200,000 miles traveling for the Campaign." It was an odd range of numbers. Retiring recording secretary Schuyler Hollingsworth, quoted on Glimp: "During the last months of the Campaign, he was probably raising most of the money himself. He had made relationships with alumni all over the country, and when the time came to close a deal people wouldn't talk to anyone else."

What the campaign did for Harvard's Faculty of Arts and Sciences, Glimp said, "was make up what the 1970s did to private universities." The damage then had been caused by inflation, a weak stock market, and greatly increased energy costs. The result, until the campaign, had been deferred maintenance and the erosion of faculty salaries. "Now," Glimp said, "we're where we were in 1974–75. That's a big gain. But it's not all done."

The level of giving had to remain near what it had risen to during the campaign, he explained. And it had to stay with the rate of inflation. "Most alumni know this. The future won't be any easier. But we have to market it differently."

The "overwhelming" portion of the campaign money came from Harvard College's fifty-eight thousand "traceable" alumni (about 45 percent of whom live in the Northeast), Tom Reardon told *The New York Times*. Area totals showed over $78 million from Boston alone, and nearly $112 million from New York City. Utah was credited with almost $126,000, the smallest state total publicized; the city of Birmingham, with over $108,000, was the smallest city total reported. One pattern of giving to the campaign symbolized the change in Harvard's demographics. There were no $15 million or $20 million gifts, but many more in the $1 million range, many given by first-time donors.

Derek Bok was leaving shortly for Florida, where he went every January. Fred Glimp was going on vacation, "to count the campaign money," his secretary joked. The custodian at Massachusetts Hall had just returned from his vacation, and it would take him at least a week, he said, as he vacuumed the front reception area, to catch up. Though classes were not in session, and many students had not yet returned for reading period (a time devoted to extra reading and writing assignments) and final exams, there was in January the usual wide assortment of special campus events, too many for anyone to keep up with. One afternoon at four o'clock in the Loeb Experimental Theatre, Susan Sontag was discussing *Jacques and His Master, An Homage to Diderot,* a play by Milan Kundera which was Sontag's first production on a U.S. stage.

Robert Stone, who'd spent the holidays in Nassau, was flying up to Boston from Florida for a meeting of the Harvard Corporation. He and Andrew Heiskell would take a helicopter back to New York together after the meeting. With those of his fellow national campaign chairmen, Albert H. Gordon and Walter N. Rothschild Jr., Stone's name was at the bottom of a letter dated January 11, 1985, that was being sent to all Harvard alumni and friends, announcing that the campaign had made its goal: "Our basic objective of keeping Harvard strong and independent has been achieved, and we can all take pride in what we have accomplished working together."

Reminiscing about the campaign, Stone spoke with visible excitement of "the guy who was rated at ten to fifty thousand, and he gives half a million." On the other hand, Stone said, with equally keen frustration, "I have some good, personal friends, whose gifts were a disappointment. You get every kind. There was an unbelievable cross section of response. By far the most generous donors were the ones who have confidence in their ability to regenerate the money for their gift. About two-thirds of the major campaign gifts were from self-made men. The toughest dollars to get were from inherited wealth."

Donors were courted, and the gifts had poured in. Five million dollars to establish a Society of Fellows in International Studies, donated by Dr. Ira Kukin, M.A. '50, Ph.D. '51. From John A. Kaneb '56, former chairman of Northeast Petroleum Industries, Inc., a gift to establish a chair in national security and military affairs; from the International Business Machines Corporation, $1 million to endow a professorship in computer science.

Less substantial but more typical than the gifts of such other major donors as Caspar W. Weinberger '38 and Donald T. Regan '40 was the contribution of $1500 by Ira Silverman '66. Silverman, who earned an M.P.A. in 1968 at the Woodrow Wilson School of Public Affairs in Princeton, where he later served as dean of admissions, was now the president of the Philadelphia-based Reconstructionist Rabbinical College. Every year since his graduation from Harvard, he had also given to the alumni fund; his wife, Jane, gave annually to Radcliffe, from which she graduated in 1967; and they both made regular contributions to Harvard's Hillel Foundation and the student social service organization Phillips Brooks House, in which they had been active as students.

With a joint annual income of about $100,000, 20 to 25 percent of which they gave to charity, the Silvermans could have afforded a larger campaign gift. But the Silvermans had never been asked for a major contribution to Harvard. And Ira Silverman, who described himself as "very emotionally attached to Harvard — Harvard Yard is *terra sancta*," believed in giving "to need rather than success."

Henry Rosovsky, sounding more and more like the patrician Bob Stone, analyzed donors who made large gifts. These donors felt they could make the money back again, he said. New money was coming in now, newly made by new donors. But the old order still ruled.

Old Money and New

No ONE, including Derek Bok, could have imagined when it was started what the Harvard Management Company would become and how important to Harvard, beyond simply managing the endowment, its role would be by the mid-1980s. In one decade, the company so stretched the definition of what Harvard University is that the disparity between reality and Harvard's public relations image of itself — as the school where the Kennedys went, where ivy grows on the brick walls, where the entire freshman class, if the admissions office so decided, could be comprised of kids with perfect SATs — that disparity is so great that it goes unacknowledged today.

Harvard needed about 330 years before its endowment reached $1 billion, "but it required more than two centuries to acquire its first million dollars," points out Seymour Harris in his 1970 monograph, *The Economics of Harvard*.

"Harvard, on the whole, has had a favorable investment history," Harris continues. "The large investments in equities in the last forty years have paid off. But there have been mistakes.

Movements into equities might have been more pronounced. Disposition of real estate after the 1929 crash was precipitate and involved costly retrievals later. In the eighteenth century, the college showed much more wisdom in tying investments to a depreciating currency than she has revealed since. The steady and costly decline of the rate of interest in the last decades of the nineteenth century were allowed to erode income without adequate reactions by Harvard's investment managers. Shifts to other investments, e.g. equities and even to real estate, might have helped. Few of the investment managers before the 1930s saw as clearly as Mr. Amos A. Laurance (1857–1862) that with inflation the policy should be a shift away from assets yielding fixed returns."

By the year Harris's book was published, a Harvard committee was reporting, "No matter how well the present arrangement has done by Harvard, it would seem appropriate for the Governing Boards to commission a careful study, by an external committee, of whether any changes should be made. We have already suggested one of the central questions: should the task of portfolio management be more sharply separated from the task of setting broad policy and reviewing performance?" Four years later, a new arrangement was in place, but whether it "more sharply separated" policy and performance was highly questionable.

Examined only in terms of its main purpose, managing Harvard's portfolio, the Harvard Management Company has transformed Harvard's finances. Conventional endowment management for nonprofit institutions seeks incremental capital growth coupled with modest earnings to pay institutional bills. Harvard, through its wholly owned subsidiary, is now a venture capitalist, a big trader, and an options player.

Though it boasts of being a leader, "breaking new ground in many previously untested and profitable investment areas," the management company in its official reports shies away from bolder proclamation. Harvard's reticence here is very real, its fear palpable. In recent years, in required filings with the Massachusetts attorney general's office, the company has left blank the space for compensation of its five highest-paid officers. The reason is symbolic of the company's success; to trumpet those figures — which the company did finally report when it was asked a second time to do so — would be to focus a bright, unwanted spotlight on a financial question that frightens Harvard more than any other. Just what constitutes its "nonprofitability"?

Despite Derek Bok's skeptical statement "that Harvard was an educational institution and had no particular skill or experience in operating an investment company," the Harvard Management Company began formal operations on July 1, 1974. When the management company was set up, Bok chaired a committee to set guidelines and goals. The major conclusions: university income would grow at 6 percent annually; endowment income growth was to be at least 6 percent, reflecting an endowment growth of 8 percent, half going to income and half to endowment, with the balance of 2 percent to be made up in gifts.

Located in the heart of Boston's downtown financial district, the management company is geographically and psychologically separated from Harvard, across the Charles River. More than a decade after its establishment, as the company's payroll climbed to one hundred people and its annual budget to over $7 million, Henry Rosovsky could mistakenly call it "distant but not crucial." Out of his sight, the company stayed out of his mind. As dean of the Faculty of Arts and Sciences, Rosovsky had overseen a departmental budget accounting for one-third of Harvard's total annual operating expenses, and he had raised millions of dollars for the Harvard Campaign. Yet his cheerful ignorance of the management company was shared by almost everyone at Harvard on the Cambridge side of the river. Its chief, Harvard treasurer George Putnam, was an enigma to them, a name associated with Harvard's endowment, and the other professionals who ran the management company were practically nonexistent.

With the sun shining onto the heads of twenty-five thousand alumni, students, parents, and professors, the President and Fellows of Harvard College were hosts for another commencement,

Harvard's 333rd. From behind the crowd, over the top hats and academic hoods, past balloons that said "Divest Now" and "Harvard Out of South Africa," Derek Bok in his robes and George Putnam and the other five fellows in their traditional morning coats made a handsome picture. Cambridge this June morning was hot. Under an off-white awning with crimson trim, behind which crimson and white banners emblazoned with Harvard's motto, Veritas, hung suspended between the pillars of Memorial Church, the seven men at center stage, perspiring from the heat, watched with vague attentiveness as the rest of the commencement procession concluded. "It's a good time to gossip," Putnam said.

Gazing at the graduates, thirty-five years after he had been one himself, Putnam felt no nostalgia on the occasion. "I didn't get a lump in my throat when they sang 'Fair Harvard,' " he said afterward. But, as the meeting was called to order by the sheriff of Middlesex County, and the prayer and first anthem were followed by the Latin salutatory oration, the senior English disquisition, and the graduate English address, and then by more music and the conferring of degrees, Putnam could recall boyhood visits to the house he saw beyond the steps of Sever Hall and the jutting corner of Emerson Hall, toward the slight elevation on the Quincy Street side of Harvard Yard.

Putnam's great-uncle, former Harvard president Abbott Lawrence Lowell, had built the house in 1911, and Lowell's successors, James Conant and Nathan Pusey, had resided there. Uncle Lawrence had been known as the builder. "During the last twenty years of his presidency," Samuel Eliot Morison wrote in *Three Centuries of Harvard*, "more new construction was completed than in all Harvard history to his day." The mammoth library, given by Mrs. George D. Widener in memory of her son Harry, Harvard '07, was built during the Lowell administration. When Derek Bok was named president, he decided to live in his own home, and 17 Quincy Street became the office of Harvard's governing boards.

The splendor of the setting was not lost on the people who

worked within it each day. They walked quietly on carpeted floors and spoke softly among themselves and when they answered the phone. But this Georgian monument to the high regard in which Harvard held itself was also a symbolic target for some. Fifteen years before, on an April day in 1969, students had gathered on its lawn in protest against the Vietnam War, and nearly a generation later, in 1985, students opposed to Harvard's investments in companies that do business in South Africa would occupy the building itself.

Except for a secretary or two and people preparing mint juleps for the president's reception, the house was empty during the commencement ceremonies. The front door was usually locked; there were many valuable paintings on the walls, and the records of the Corporation were guarded as if they were state secrets. Inside, to the right of a huge hallway, was a ballroom with two crystal chandeliers and a high mantel over a fireplace where George Putnam once played parlor games with his Uncle Lawrence before being put to bed on Christmas Eve.

There is a photograph, taken a few years ago at a Harvard commencement, showing the march of procession past University Hall. President Bok and the university marshal are just beginning the turn around the end of the building — they have already passed the statue of John Harvard — and behind the president, who is wearing his academic robes, is George Putnam in his top hat and morning coat. Each of the other fellows of Harvard College seems to be looking at someone in the crowd that is standing to either side of the procession, and the looks are a mix of vacant stares, wary glances, and quizzical reflections. George Putnam appears to be looking straight at the photographer, his eyes set above a wide, straight, close-mouthed grin. Midsection, before the buttons of his vest, he has clasped his hands, almost in a cupping position, as someone might if he were about to twiddle his thumbs. There is also, in the half of his right knee showing behind Bok's robes, a hint in the angle and the height that Putnam is not just walking but really marching.

"His swinging style," Derek Bok was now saying of Benny

Goodman to the commencement multitudes who had been waiting for this moment, "and melodic improvisation have lifted the hearts and feet of generations of Americans." A standing ovation followed the presentation to Goodman of an honorary degree. In other parts of Harvard Yard children played tag and the class marshals assembled for a photograph. A small cluster of alumni sipped soft drinks on the steps of Weld Hall, where one of the reunion classes was signing in that day for a long weekend of formalized nostalgia.

Shortly, after the Harvard hymn and the benediction, the President and Fellows of Harvard College, the honorands, and the overseers recessed down the center aisle toward Widener Library, and the sheriff adjourned the meeting. The Harvard University Band played "Old Comrades March." Journalists snapped pictures of Goodman, or two of his fellow honorary-degree recipients, Barbara Tuchman and King Juan Carlos I, or Derek Bok. No one paid special attention to Putnam, nor was he recognized by anyone save his friends and family. Many years before, Putnam had chosen a life of professional anonymity, and even within Harvard he was a mystery man. People knew his name, but most had no idea what he did. Practically no one at the Harvard Management Company knew him personally.

George Putnam had stayed on as Harvard's treasurer long enough. There were grumblings among his colleagues on the Harvard Corporation that he didn't spend enough time, was out of touch, didn't understand the rapidly changing financial world of which Harvard was a part. Harvard, so the case against Putnam went, needed a treasurer who was *there*. And who could hold his tongue. George Putnam, some people thought, talked too much.

If you had asked him about this, Putnam might have given a quizzical look, or he might have smiled, but he certainly would not have replied in kind. He liked to say he had a thick skin. And he believed he knew, far better than his detractors, what made Harvard work. He had a sense of the place, steeped in family history and his own experience, that transcended someone else's concern over the intricacies of Harvard's financial policies or the routine management of its affairs. Described by David Aloian as "one of the best pro bono people in Boston," Putnam also had an extraordinary confidence in himself, a certainty about who he was and what he could do, and few people with whom he worked got close to him.

"Once, my wife and I went to a hockey game with George and Barbara after a dinner we had together," said Aloian. "We had a lot in common then at Harvard, and George was on the board of the St. Mark's School when I was headmaster of Belmont Hill. We were on the board of McLean [Hospital]. But we don't go fishing together."

With an allusion to the past, when Harvard's treasurer had been an appointee of the Massachusetts governor, Putnam referred to himself as "the independent treasurer," relishing with an almost mischievous grin a realization of the way this must have rankled Derek Bok, who commanded complete loyalty from his own administrators. Putnam had great respect for Bok, but he was not awed by him. It *was* time for him to move on, but he had made that decision himself, thank you.

Putnam was born in 1926 in Manchester, a coastal town north of Boston, incorporated in 1645 and fondly called by the locals Manchester-by-the-Sea. Situated on the underside of a peninsula that, at its tip, forms Cape Ann, the town encompasses some of the most valuable real estate in New England. Its pretty harbor, which sometimes freezes over during the winter, and alluring spots with descriptive names like Singing Beach long ago began attracting the summer crowd. Manchester has lost any semblance it once had to an old fishing village. Several diplomats have lived there; Christian Herter, secretary of state from 1959 to 1961, was once a Putnam neighbor. Henry Hobson Richardson designed the town's library; correct Manchesterians play golf and tennis together at the Essex County Club, where Harvard's twenty-fifth reunion classes gather each year; and in the 1980s, with a population of about five thousand, Manchester is a place where, if something needs repair — say the steeple of the Congregational church — it is fixed properly and promptly.

Conjuring a quaint image of a pleasant street in a tidy neighborhood, George Putnam would tell you he lived now in the house next door to the one in which he grew up. This was a true statement as far as it went, but what it left out was misleading. Putnam's boyhood home — or one of them, for the family spent part of each year in Boston — was of a scale and style that, in touristy Newport, would have put it on a sightseer's map. Mansion was a better word for it. With its gabled roof, large center porch with iron railings and twin smaller porches on either side, facing down toward a terrace and pool below, it looked out on an inlet of the Atlantic Ocean called Lobster Cove. A wide expanse of sloping lawn, with maples and pines, separated the stately brick building from the smaller, rambling "summer cottage" in which Putnam's cousins, the Bundys, had lived, and where Putnam and his wife, Barbara, moved in the 1950s to raise their own family. These sylvan surroundings were a second skin to him, but Putnam, whose reserve in such matters was habitual and usually unwavering, was engagingly proprietary and would urge overnight guests to arrive early. The estate and the orchids he grew there were, he could not resist admitting, "best seen in the daylight."

Putnam was old money and old Boston and old Harvard. Putnam's grandmother had been a Lowell; his Uncle Lawrence had been her brother, while her other brother was the astronomer Percival Lowell and a sister the poet Amy Lowell. They were Uncle Percy and Aunt Amy to Putnam, though both had died before his birth. "Right-o," he might reply, in the clipped Boston accent that bore traces of Maine, to a question confirming their relation to him. There were so many such relatives that he wasn't even certain how close he was to all of them. He and Robert Lowell, he said, "were not very far apart," but that was as well as he could do to define his kinship with the great poet. The feigned disinterest could be disarming to a stranger, and Putnam wasn't above casually dropping a name at a strategic point in conversation. No further, substantive information was proffered spontaneously, but if he were prompted Putnam would go on at length, with references to Pilgrims and asides about assorted other famous family folk, including the "first" George Putnam, who was the present George's great-great-grandfather. That Putnam had been the clergyman of the First Church in Roxbury, Massachusetts, where John Amory Lowell was a parishioner. Both men had graduated from Harvard — Rev. Putnam in 1826 and Lowell in 1815 — and by the time of the Civil War both were fellows on the Harvard Corporation; Lowell, in fact, was the senior fellow. He served Harvard for forty years, and it was his grandson, Abbott Lawrence Lowell, who succeeded Charles William Eliot as president in 1909.

Putnam's father — another George — was a prominent Boston financier. In 1937 he organized the George Putnam Fund of Boston, a mutual fund that, nearly half a century later, was one of twenty-three managed by the Putnam Management Company, Inc. The company, of which George *fils* had been chairman since 1970, supervised institutional and mutual fund assets that by early 1985 exceeded $13 billion (about half of which were assets of the mutual funds).

Putnam went to prep school at St. Mark's and in 1944 enlisted in the air force. The war was over before he saw action, and he entered Harvard in 1945. "I wasn't close to Harvard as an undergraduate," Putnam said. He remembered it as "a mixed-up time," with many students returning from military duty. There was little class cohesiveness and identity; Robert F. Kennedy, Putnam's kindergarten classmate at Boston's School for Little Beavers, was a member of the Class of 1948, while Putnam graduated magna cum laude in 1949. He would later defeat Kennedy in election to Harvard's Board of Overseers. That was in 1967, long after Putnam had earned an M.B.A. at Harvard Business School and then gone to work in 1951 for his family's investment business ("to please my father, whose health was failing rapidly"). Kennedy, Putnam recalled, took the overseer defeat well. "Before Harvard notified me that I'd won, I received a telegram from Bobby congratulating me," he said. John F. Kennedy had run for overseer, too, and, said Putnam, "he didn't make it the first time he was on the ballot either." Later, when Kennedy was both a Harvard overseer and president of the United States, the board once met at the White House. Talking about the Kennedys, Putnam referred to them in familiar terms; Robert Kennedy was always Bobby, and the late president was Jack.

Putnam refers to himself as a farmer-sailor. He spends as many weekends as he can in an old farmhouse on Mount Desert Island in Maine, where he is his own carpenter, plumber, and electrician. The Maine farmhouse, built in 1834, was moved to its present site after being unoccupied for about fifty years, and Putnam did all the renovation work himself. It is a five-hour drive from Manchester to the island, and Putnam once considered buying an airplane and learning how to fly to make the trip a shorter one. But landing a plane in Maine's fog is tricky, and Putnam likes to drive. "It's my thinking time," he says. "I don't have a fancy car" (he owns a Chevy Cavalier) "but I do have a tape player." He records his own cassettes, which range from the classics to the Boston Pops, and near the end of a journey rewards himself with what he calls "some sugar candy — a Broadway musical."

Mounted on a wall behind the large desk in Putnam's ninth-floor corner office at One Post Office Square — headquarters of Putnam Management — was a dartboard. It was a humorous representation of how important investment decisions were made, and Putnam invited visitors to share the joke. But the fact that it was hanging there at all symbolized something else. As Harvard's treasurer since 1973, Putnam held the most powerful financial position at the nation's oldest and richest university. His fiscal authority was second only to that of President Bok, and in many cases independent of Bok's. Like Bok, he was both governor and administrator. As treasurer, he was a member of the Harvard Corporation, which was charged with Harvard's fiduciary responsibility, but also as treasurer, Putnam oversaw the administration of Harvard's endowment. That work required more than the use of a dartboard, but Putnam never seemed to lose a sense of humor about himself, nor a modesty about the role he played in modernizing Harvard's financial affairs. "I consider it a great privilege not to have spent all my time in the commercial world," was how he put it once. "My order of priorities is: one, family; two, someone who pays me for my time; three, charity; and four, someone looking for advice."

Implicit in the understatement that was characteristic of his speech was the assumption of peerage with anyone of respectable wealth or renown. Not everyone, finding himself in similar company, would have employed the economy of language, expressive of such genteel egalitarianism, to describe his colleagues on the Harvard Corporation, who included the retired chairman of Time Inc. and the commodore of the New York Yacht Club, as did Putnam. "Nifty," he called them, and in the choice of this single adjective was a revelation of the quality that made some people uncomfortable with him. He intimidated certain people, not because he was wealthy, not because he was intelligent, not because he believed and acted as if manners mattered, and not because he was good at what he did, but through the genuine impression he conveyed of a person who was supremely content, whose happiness came not from the satisfaction of doing his job but of living his life. His good cheer and abundant energy frightened others. He seemed invulnerable to the common concerns of his fellow men. He was disinterested; the trick for Putnam wasn't so much in what he had but in how he used it. He seemed unafraid to admit an ignorance, to acknowledge a debt, to make a new acquaintance. His involvement in the moment was total, his concentration on what was at hand complete. George Putnam was in love with his world.

But not everyone in that world loved Putnam. "Putnam," said

Hale Champion, Harvard's financial vice president when Putnam became treasurer, "is the most genial ass-coverer . . ." He let the phrase dangle and didn't complete it. Other, more timid souls, who would not criticize him on the record, spoke of Putnam's being spread too thin, of his lacking depth. The most serious charges were that Putnam wouldn't close ranks publicly when a problem surfaced and that Putnam couldn't keep up with all the complexities of the university's investment management. Options trading, for example, at which the Harvard Management Company specialized, was simply too sophisticated to be understood by a treasurer with his own business interests to supervise and with as many other corporate and nonprofit board commitments to keep as Putnam had.

Harvard's independent treasurer did get around. His official biography, which listed primarily the present highlights of a lifetime of such service, read in part: "He is a Governor and past Chairman of the Investment Company Institute; he serves on the boards of American Mutual Insurance Co., The Boston Company, Inc., Boston Safe Deposit and Trust Company, Freeport-McMoran, Inc., General Mills, Inc., Rockefeller Group, Inc., and American Public Radio. He is currently a Trustee of the Massachusetts General Hospital, The Colonial Williamsburg Foundation, Museum of Fine Arts, Boston, The Nature Conservancy, The Jackson Laboratory, a Member of the Massachusetts Educational Loan Authority and a member of the faculty of the Museum of Comparative Zoology of Harvard. . . . He is also a past Trustee of Bradford College, Boston Museum of Science, the New England Aquarium, Massachusetts Horticultural Society and the Manchester Public Library." Brief mention was made of his having been a Wellesley trustee, but none of his being a trustee of St. Mark's or president of the McLean Hospital Board of Trustees. He was, the biography duly noted, "President and Chairman of each of the Putnam Funds, and Director of The Putnam Advisory Company, Inc. and Putnam Financial Services, Inc." And he was "married to the former Barbara Weld, Wellesley AB '49. Their children are George, III, Harvard AB '73 (MCL), MBA '78; Barbara P. Lyman, Harvard '76; and Susan W. Putnam, Harvard '79 (C.L.)." Small stylistic touches here seemed expressive of Putnam: the use of uppercase letters to begin the words *president, chairman,* and *director,* and the inclusion, without definition, of "MCL" and "C.L.," standing for magna cum laude and cum laude, signified a subtle respect for rank, which by a never mentioned word meant class. The tiny typing discrepancy in the presence of periods in "C.L." and their absence in "MCL" gave the paper the appearance that it hadn't been proofread.

During days when he could have dined at his choice of Boston's most expensive restaurants, Putnam would help himself to a salad in the small Putnam Management Company dining area down the hall from his office. He would pass up the chocolate chip cookies and carry his salad on a tray back to his office. There was nothing exotic about going out to eat, and, like proofing one's biography — or playing golf, or gambling, or smoking, so many silly things — it was such a waste of time.

Harvard business occupied him regularly, and he spoke of his alma mater with personal affection. He always would. His Harvard address — he never had an office there — was also in Boston, at 70 Federal Street. There, on four floors of a small building tucked between the skyscrapers that house the city's major banks, were the headquarters of the Harvard Management Company, where several of the most complicated giving programs for alumni were tied into the management of a donor's assets by the company. The company was headed by Walter Cabot, Harvard '55, who once worked for the Putnam Management Company, and whose family was one of Boston's and Harvard's most illustrious. His uncle, Paul C. Cabot '21, had served Harvard as treasurer and manager of the endowment from 1948 to 1965, and numerous other Cabots had gone to Harvard and been generous benefactors.

Such close familial and corporate ties were common at Harvard. The incorporation papers for the Harvard Management Company were drawn up by a Harvard alumnus at the university's legal counsel, Ropes & Gray, an old, prestigious Boston firm founded by a Harvard Law School professor, John Chipman Gray, Harvard Class of 1859. There, one of the senior partners was Putnam's friend, Hooks Burr, also an alumnus and for twenty-eight years, until 1982, a member of the Harvard Corporation. Burr was also a director of the Harvard Management Company. The offices of Ropes & Gray were in the State Street Bank building, a block from Putnam's offices. The web of relationships was dizzying, and it touched many other aspects of Harvard's governance, finance, and administration, including the Harvard Campaign.

Putnam watched the campaign operations from the sidelines, but as treasurer he was very much involved in the process once a donation had been made. Under Putnam's supervision, Assistant Treasurer Henry Ameral accepted gifts at the Harvard Management Company, where new funds were immediately invested. But not all gifts were monetary, and Putnam was the final arbiter when there was a question about whether Harvard would accept donations of a vacation home in Hawaii or a collection of rare wines.

Putnam himself had made a contribution to the campaign — actually several, a series of charitable lead trusts, with a total value of over $1 million. He thus joined a very select group of donors whose campaign gifts were in seven figures. Forty-five of their names were printed in an issue of *The Harvard Campaign Report,* followed by a group represented by the word "Anonymous." Overall, there were eighty-two such large gifts — sixty in the $1 million to $2 million range, twelve in the $2 million to $5 million range, eight between $5 million and $10 million, and two others that together totaled $18 million. Prominent among the donors were former secretary of the treasury Douglas Dillon, David Rockefeller, Karim Aga Khan, former chairman of CBS Frank Stanton, and Dr. An Wang.

By the fall of 1984, when the Harvard Campaign had needed $22 million to reach its goal, Putnam could raise one of his thick eyebrows and look with some skepticism at the possibility of the campaign's falling short. "They held some gifts back," Putnam said later. The suspense had been something of a put-on. He could also point out that "Harvard has worked hard to make itself a national university." One consequence of that, Putnam continued, was a sense among certain Bostonians that Harvard was no longer "theirs." Putnam, a tall man with wavy graying hair, with a smile that was framed above by high cheekbones and below by an angular jaw, realized that Harvard was now a place very unlike the one he had known as a boy.

Putnam, who took particular pleasure in making small, hard-to-trace gifts to such favorite Harvard causes of his as the university's obscure sailing program, laughed about the published gift list. Pretending modesty, he said, "When the newsletter came out, my wife said, 'Hide all your copies, George, before the children see you there.' " Like his predecessors, Putnam quietly practiced another form of gift giving. Each year during his term as treasurer, he turned back to Harvard his annual salary, which had reached about $60,000 for part-time work. He did this without fanfare, unbeknownst to Derek Bok.

But, then, there was a lot Bok didn't know about Putnam, including Putnam's personal feelings about the president. Putnam was the only key administrator Bok hadn't selected. Putnam had, in fact, been the head of the search committee that ended up selecting himself, and he'd accepted the position almost as a favor, or so he maintained. "I'm very fond of Bok," said Putnam, and right away, again in the choice of a word, he was showing more than he should. There were many styles of speaking about Bok at Harvard, and they ran the full range of opinion, but no one else used such a word as *fond,* as though the president were a nice chap who had worked hard and finally earned the praise of a person who's been keeping an eye on him.

"Bok," Putnam continued in his assessment, "is shy, a loner, afraid of being too gregarious. Derek's a little afraid of his own shadow. He doesn't stick his neck out on appointments." Thinking about the Monday meetings of the Corporation, Putnam said the president was "great for having material to us in advance." It would arrive on a Friday, and it was two to three inches thick. Barbara Putnam called the two days that followed her husband's Harvard weekends.

Putnam never would have agreed to be president of the management company. It would have severely cramped his style, and he would have been bored by the details he would have had to take care of. As treasurer, he reviewed results. That way he could be "hard-nosed." Putnam was so relaxed as he said this, so trusting that his meaning was clear, you couldn't conceive of a subordinate's crossing him. The long stare expressing hurt more than anger would be too painful.

He could be equally candid talking about his "good friend," former Massachusetts governor Edward King, a framed citation from whom hung on Putnam's office wall. "Ed's very self-confident," he said, "which is why he was always saying things that got him into trouble." With a reference to MATEP, the power plant that had cost Harvard millions more than had been anticipated and that was chiefly responsible for Harvard's huge debt, Putnam said King "was a godsend. Just plain helpful." You weren't supposed to say things like this at Bok's Harvard, where avoidance of candor was a virtue. The world was waiting to pounce on Harvard, and you shouldn't give it ammunition.

As an overseer, Putnam had served on a committee that had, he said, "studied what had gone wrong in the sixties. It was an unusually interesting time," he continued. "I was in the last group of overseers for a time who could be elected from the business community. Did I have a sense of what I was getting into? None! I found the overseers more interesting than being on the Corporation. The overseers were well informed. The Corporation gets stuff thrown at them, it was concerned with the trees but missed the forest. That's changed much in the past few years.

Yes, there's some friction between the groups, particularly from among overseers who've served as trustees elsewhere."

Further random observations were made in an omnipotent tone. There were no gray areas in Putnam's views of Harvard:

"I believe the Harvard treasurer is an overseer. He represents the money Harvard already has.

"I feel strongly that Harvard should be in the black, and that we should do honest bookkeeping — you can't cheat on maintenance, you must take regular depreciation every year.

"Like the United States government, Harvard takes a lot of capitalized expenses as operating expenses.

"A good corporation keeps track of everything. Harvard keeps track of almost everything.

"Being on the Corporation is fun. You meet interesting people. And it's a way of having something in common with your children who are in school."

Putnam's three children were grown up now, living elsewhere, and the Putnams didn't need so much space. Perhaps, when they were younger, he and Barbara had assumed they would move someday into the brick house. His mother was ninety-three. On a January morning, the view from his own home, as the sky began to lighten and far across the gray ocean water a line of sun-color appeared, could be forbidding: beyond this winter park, away from Barbara Putnam's rock garden and the greenhouses, beyond the sculptured stillness of the ice-covered pond below the pool, the ocean beckoned with a relentless prod to the imagination. It was a view that invited one to leave this protected place, to rule the world beyond the water (as had George Putnam's cousins, William and McGeorge Bundy, who had grown up in the house where George Putnam lived), and to join the CIA or become the national security adviser to the president. Instead, professing loyalty to family, community, and college, Putnam had remained home. He had no need of headlines to satisfy his ambition, and he understood that power is exercised privately as well as publicly.

It was very cold this January morning. The day before, wearing a trench coat over his gray suit, Putnam had said good night to his secretary, Nancy Boardman, who after working for him for twenty years still calls him Mr. Putnam, and left his office at One Post Office Square about 6 P.M. He'd already checked the market; the Dow Jones industrial average was up 11.04 points, and the prices for all but one of the mutual funds managed by Putnam Management Company would show an increase in the next morning's newspapers. Putnam's car was parked in its usual spot, the basement garage of the State Street Bank building in downtown Boston. There was a theater program for *42nd Street* in the back seat. Driving the car out of the garage, Putnam turned the wrong way onto a one-way street to avoid having to go around the block. "I always do it," he said. "Someday I'll get smashed."

That afternoon, during a dull meeting of one of the many boards he was on, Putnam had sketched a driveway plan for the new house he and Barbara Putnam planned to build on the family property in Manchester. Putnam had previously sketched those plans, too, but an architect needed to go over them before any construction began. The drive from Boston to his home could take as long as an hour, but this evening the bridge traffic out of the city wasn't bad, and Putnam was soon headed north on Route 1 to Route 128 east.

The next week he would be in Los Angeles on Putnam Management Company business, before flying to Hawaii to give a talk about an Indonesian gold mine to a group that had invited him to speak a year and a half ago. His wife was traveling with him. He was "enormously relieved" that he'd "gotten out" of having also to go to Tokyo before returning home. But he never complained about all the travel. He liked flying. "I get my briefcase work done," he said.

"I don't know what I accomplished today," he continued, "but I was busy."

Putnam was met at the front door of his house by his younger daughter, Susan, who lived in Cambridge. She had come by to pick up a few things before leaving with a friend for a vacation in Acapulco. "Stay away longer and come over to Hawaii with us," her father said. They stood talking in the hallway for ten or fifteen minutes, Putnam keeping his hands in his pants pockets and swaying slightly on the balls of his feet, in a pose reminiscent of Robert F. Kennedy. Putnam looked very trim; he had a small waist, with no fat or flab. When it was time for Susan to go, she opened the door and walked out; there was no fuss about good-byes, no last hug and kiss.

Barbara Putnam was wearing a pink sweater and a woolen skirt. She had played tennis that day. Before dinner, both Putnams had bourbon, George mixing his. Dinner was filet of sole, the wine a Soave white. No coffee for George with dessert, which was apple cobbler with Brigham's vanilla ice cream.

"Anne Pusey was such a great hostess," Barbara Putnam said during dinner, speaking of the wife of Harvard's previous president. Mrs. Putnam was once on a Harvard committee that had studied the university's food service, she said. She did her own cooking and had no live-in servants. She and her husband communicated with each other by gesture as well as word. When it was time to leave the table, nothing was said. Silently, a signal was given, and Barbara disappeared into the kitchen to clean the dishes. George doted on her without being demonstrative. His interest in her activities was unaffected and complete. Listening to the brief report of her tennis match, he focused totally on the topic, as though for that moment its importance transcended anything else in his hectic life. It did.

The talk turned to Maine. As a young man, George remembered fighting the famous fire on Cadillac Mountain. Just that day, he had received in the mail a monthly electric bill for $8 from Maine. The farmer he "shared" with a neighbor must have been doing some work at the house, he concluded. He seemed quite concerned that the bill was too high and had been carrying it around with him in his coat pocket. He thought he might go to Maine for the weekend. Mrs. Putnam looked up and said she wasn't sure if she would.

Putnam's father and Samuel Eliot Morison had been next-door neighbors on Mount Desert Island. Their summer homes there were about half a mile apart.

"Morison used to be suspicious of my father," said Putnam, "because he was a businessman. But one day Morison walked over and found my father napping, with a copy of Plutarch's *Lives* in his lap, and they became friends after that.

"You know, Morison wrote most of his naval histories in his boat, which was anchored offshore. When I was a boy, I used to sail my dinghy in the bay there, and I knew not to disturb him. But he told me, if I saw smoke coming from the smokestack, that meant he'd finished his day's work, and I could come on board and have a bowl of porridge with him."

Putnam took Morison's Harvard course in naval history. The day of the first class, Morison asked two women students to leave. "He said he didn't want them to hear some of his navy stories," Putnam recalled. "It would embarrass them to hear them. And it would embarrass him to tell them. I was thrown out of his class myself once. I thought maybe it was because I was wearing a pink shirt — they were just becoming popular then. I asked the admiral afterwards if that were the reason. 'No,' he said. 'You weren't wearing a coat and tie.' "

More stories — Putnam had a story to tell about everyone he knew: another great-uncle of Putnam's, Professor Oakes Ames of the Harvard Botany Department, was involved in a celebrated dispute over Harvard's custody of the Arnold Arboretum, established in 1872 through the bequest to Harvard of land and a trust fund by James Arnold. In 1945, Harvard proposed that most of the arboretum's library and its dried herbs be moved to Cambridge, and the resulting fuss was not resolved until a 1967 decision in Harvard's favor by the Massachusetts Supreme Judicial Court. Ames, an orchidologist who had for a time directed the arboretum, was one of several prominent figures who sided against Harvard in the struggle, which by the time of George Putnam's graduation from Harvard was so bitter that one member of the Harvard Corporation resigned the following year.

Putnam, whose undergraduate degree was in biochemistry, was an orchidologist himself. At one time, he had intended to make biochemistry his career, before his father interceded. His wife, too, was a horticulturalist, and Putnam has built several greenhouses at their Manchester home, three of which house his collection of several hundred orchids. During his years as a Harvard overseer, Putnam was chairman of the visiting committee to the Arnold Arboretum.

George and Barbara Putnam rarely ate anymore in the dining room they'd added to the house, with the oil portrait of Putnam's grandfather and another painting Putnam described as "half a Tintoretto" on the walls. A sleeping porch off the living room wasn't heated, and the old Brunswick pool table there was kept covered. "I paid twenty-five or fifty bucks for it," Putnam said. "Now they sell remakes for eighteen thousand." There were orchids everywhere, on tables in the living room and den, in a small greenhouse off the coat closet, and in a larger greenhouse off the basement. Putnam's Sunday morning routine included the weekly watering of his plants.

The family room Putnam had added off the dining room had a parquet floor, which he had laid himself. There was a record collection Putnam pointed out, and a slide projector was set up in the middle of the room. There were many leather-bound books in the small room George called the library. Among the volumes were the complete works of James Russell Lowell, another relative. Next to the color television and Sears VCR was a stack of book-shaped cases for videotapes, including "Jane Fonda's Workout."

Two standard poodles named Molly and Fancy had the run of the house. Because the furniture in the living room was white, the living room doors were closed to keep the dogs out when the Putnams went to bed shortly before midnight, after Putnam had watched the television weather report. He was still wearing the clothes he'd come home in, never having taken off the coat to his suit.

The following morning, breakfasting on orange juice, an English muffin with apricot marmalade, and a glass of low-fat milk, Putnam told his wife he'd be staying at the Union League while he was in New York City overnight. He would fly to New York, where he went one or two days a week, on the afternoon shuttle. He ignored the morning newspaper that had been brought inside by a local high school student and excused himself to pack his bag, which was so small that it could not have contained more than a clean shirt and toiletries. He had remembered to wear a tie with Boston College colors because he was seeing an alumnus of that school at a meeting later.

The temperature that night had gone down almost to zero. A car was parked by the garage apartment to his mother's house, which some years ago, Putnam said, had "lost" seventeen rooms. "Mother had them chopped off." The homes of a few neighbors were visible through the stark winter foliage, but there was no one around as Putnam guided his car up the winding driveway and onto the quiet street.

In town, he nodded toward the new firehouse, mentioning that he'd served on Manchester's finance committee. He'd had "a deal" with his board, Putnam explained, that he could take on four not-for-profit and four for-profit outside activities. "I've enjoyed both," he said. "It's allowed me to travel a lot. I like to vary things, for the most part turning things over regularly. When one of the companies is bought, my friends say, 'Isn't that a tragedy.' And I say, 'No, it's great for the shareholders, and I can go on to something else.'"

Putnam had "gotten out" of a few of the less glamorous boards on which he served when he took the Harvard treasurer's job in 1973. It had been a good excuse for that. "I left an even dozen," he said. It was not unlike the way some people he knew "went to Washington" — something he hadn't done — went there, he said, because it was a way of wiping the slate clean and being able to start over on one's return.

When Putnam had accepted appointment as Harvard's treasurer, it was his understanding and Harvard's that Putnam's commitment would be half time. A year later, the Harvard Management Company began operations. Derek Bok knew too little about investments to monitor what Putnam did, nor would Putnam have stood for someone's looking over his shoulder. But Putnam, a full-time Brahmin and a half-time treasurer, was too busy to keep a close eye on the management company, which had grown not just in size but in complexity and sophistication. For Putnam, being Harvard's treasurer was like serving on Manchester's finance committee. It was the decent thing to do, a favor to an old friend.

Putnam left the day-to-day decision making and supervision to someone else. With his extraordinary charm and self-confidence, he looked for certain qualities in other people that he could exploit to his advantage and Harvard's. Among those people, one man stood out, his ambitious young assistant and Harvard's associate treasurer, George Siguler. Though he never indulged in hyperbole when talking about him, Putnam held Siguler in great affection. "He isn't a genius," Putnam said. But Siguler "can explain Harvard's use of options, futures, stock lending, bond immunization and special situations well or better than anyone in Boston. He initiated most of these programs."

Pausing late one day outside his office, Putnam shook his head and smiled, savoring the image of the kid from Cleveland who'd taken a new, undefined job at Harvard for a relative pittance and eventually earned more money than the highest-paid professor. "He isn't a line-man," Putnam said, meaning Siguler didn't work on the nuts and bolts of a program. "That would be a waste of his talents." Putnam's smile broadened, as a father's might, praising his son. Siguler, Putnam confessed, "got away with murder!"

*

An only child, George W. Siguler lost his father when he was twelve. "We were as poor as could be," he recalls. He went to a public high school in his hometown, Cleveland, and did well enough to be accepted by Amherst College on early decision. He enrolled there in September 1965 and almost immediately fell behind in his work. In one course, where forty was the minimum grade usually given by the professor, he received a thirty-eight. At the end of his freshman year, Siguler says, the Amherst dean of students "asked me to leave the college and come back after I'd served my country."

Siguler, who was upset but "had no hard feelings" about what had happened (Amherst regularly did this then with students who weren't performing well) enlisted in the naval reserve. After boot camp, he was assigned to duty on a ship, where he hurt his back. Honorably discharged, he immediately returned to Amherst to speak with the dean.

"He told me it was too soon to come back," Siguler says, "so I went home to Cleveland and got a job with what was still the New York Central Railroad. They put me to work in the accounting office. There weren't any computers, and everything was done manually. I had to learn the hard way to do twenty-eight-column ledgers." The following fall, he was readmitted to Amherst, and when the college heard of Siguler's accounting experience, he was given a part-time job reconciling the fraternity books. "I had to make sure the liquor stores got paid," says Siguler. "And I did! The stores used to give me free liquor." By this time, Siguler had also started playing the stock market — "just a little." He finished Amherst in January 1970 and took a job in the claims department of the Springfield, Massachusetts, office of Aetna Insurance Company while he waited to hear from the business schools to which he had applied. The last school to accept him — that June — was Harvard, and he enrolled in the fall. "Apparently, they forgot about my freshman year at Amherst."

Before he'd completed his M.B.A. two years later, Siguler

took a course in university administration, and he wrote a paper for the course on managing an endowment. He became an investment analyst in Minneapolis with a large mutual funds company, Investors Diversified Services (IDS), but he retained his interest in endowments. One day the subject came up in a conversation with the head of investments at IDS, who suggested Siguler call Putnam.

"You'll be needing some help," Siguler said to Putnam.

Putnam replied that he'd already received piles of material from people who wanted to give him that help. "But if you're ever in Boston, come by and we'll meet."

The way Siguler looked at it, "even the downside was positive"; if he weren't offered a job, speaking with Putnam would still help his work at IDS. He flew to Boston for an interview. As he waited outside Putnam's office, he said to Putnam's secretary, Nancy Boardman, "I sure hope he likes me."

Putnam did. The two men, twenty years apart in age and from totally different backgrounds, hit it off. Putnam had taken the Harvard job only on the condition that it would be half time. He was already finalizing plans for establishing a company to manage Harvard's portfolio, and he would need someone who understood the investment business and could be his surrogate during the times he wasn't present. A few weeks later, he called Siguler and offered him a position as his assistant. The job meant a pay cut for Siguler, who had just turned twenty-six, but he took it. The decision changed his life. And Siguler's relationship with Putnam, which soon blossomed into full friendship, changed Harvard's finances.

Siguler has a high-pitched voice, varying widely in tone from the registration of keen interest to complete boredom. He talks very quickly, often impatiently, but he listens well. His physical presence is intense; he seems always to be thinking about several things at once, and there is a kind of nervous tic to the way he sits or stands in conversation. He remarks with amazement at the idea of someone's living what he sees as an unstructured life, implying that he needs the goals and rewards of the financial world to get himself going each day. Not having to be at the office, not having an audience to respond immediately to what one says or does would be anathema to him. He quit smoking cigarettes long ago, quit his pipe later. He is adamantly opposed to smoking now, freely dispensing unsolicited advice to a smoker in his presence.

He cares greatly about rank. Past associates are invariably mentioned as "having worked under or for me." He has an incessant need to remind his listener of the famous and important people he knows. Among his many friends is one of the owners of the Boston Red Sox. He attended a game in 1984 with the reclusive Jean Yawkey, president of the team, sitting in her private box. However, points out one of the people who calls Siguler occasionally for advice, "If you ask one of those people about George, they have only the best to say about him." He is also fond of perks, even remembering to mention the parking sticker he had as an Amherst student that permitted him to park his car anywhere on campus.

Siguler, says a consultant to the management company, "is an intrinsically low-risk guy. He makes some bets that others won't, but what he invented were things that don't have risks in themselves but have powerful capabilities."

Dean A. Michael Spence, who as chairman of the Advisory Committee on Shareholder Responsibility worked sometimes with Siguler, called him "very creative, an idea a minute, some off the wall, but well worth the price."

Derek Bok believed Siguler had a "special role as a special young person. . . . He contributed a high quantity of new ideas." Such a person, Bok continued, "was always going to be unsettling to other people." Their "inevitable, periodic frustrations and disagreements were healthy. People like familiar practices. Who knows, maybe someday George Siguler will be treasurer of Harvard."

Siguler and the management company prospered under Putnam. The endowment doubled in value. When MATEP cost overruns threatened to throw Harvard's budget out of balance, Siguler came to the rescue with a brilliant bond strategy. Many of the largest campaign gifts to Harvard were trusts the company managed. Putnam had given Siguler and the company free rein. He'd had no choice, considering his other commitments. But he'd covered for himself. When he had to know something, when Derek Bok asked him a question about security lending or options trading he couldn't answer, he got the answer from Siguler.

Siguler says he attended "probably every other Corporation meeting" while he worked at Harvard. Sometimes, he'd have breakfast with Bob Stone. He calls the Board of Overseers "irrelevant." He didn't think Harvard fund raisers did enough, were creative enough, in fund raising. They ought to, he thought, take books being discarded from the library, inscribe them, send them to donors — things like that, little things. Once, he helped Fred Glimp with the gift of some land in Seattle. The two men flew out to look it over and meet with the donors, who were not alumni. Several years later, the property had been sold and the proceeds credited to the Harvard Campaign.

"I think," said George Putnam, "Siguler may feel — you know his father died when he was very young — so he may feel he only has a limited time to do what he wants to do."

George Siguler and his wife, Pam, visit the Putnam place in Maine every summer for five or six days. Putnam built a modern A-frame near the water ("that must have been before the environmentalists were active," says Siguler) and the Sigulers stay in that when they go.

"We do what we want," says Siguler. "But George might say in the afternoon, 'Would you like to help me fix a fence?' He's always doing something. We see him riding around in his tractor. Sometimes we talk shop. The plan to break up the equities into portfolios at the management company was hatched while we cut hay by hand with sickles. George is like a father and brother to me. And I've never heard him swear or seen him lose his cool."

Never actually responsible himself for the routine management of Harvard money — that would have been too confining and repetitious — Siguler was instead a strategist, a prodder of portfolio managers and analysts, and a go-between, with his colleagues at the management company on one end and George Putnam at the other. His mind was an endless source of new ideas, and he had the force of personality to fight for them. When he wanted to do something, he didn't worry about authority, because he had something the others didn't: access. He was Putnam's man, and everyone knew it.

"Siguler," says one of the people who worked with him, "is a product of the American business scene. He combines ability with social instincts." Siguler put that combination to work very quickly at Harvard. He dressed well — pinstripe suits and button-down shirts — drove a sports car, and bought a Back Bay condominium, which he would later sell to buy a farmhouse in Weston. He cultivated his relationship with Harvard's rich and powerful and was soon on a first-name basis with most of them. Putnam asked him to assist in the selection of a president for the management company. There were over one hundred candidates who were seriously considered, and the search committee's list was pared down to five during a meeting in Florida by a group that included Siguler and Putnam. Siguler was helping to choose his boss.

"I was down there at a place about half a mile from Putnam," Siguler says, "so we got together. I remember walking barefoot on Pompano Beach with George. That was really the start of our relationship." The man eventually chosen for the job was Walter Cabot, who had been working for the Putnam Management Company when George Siguler was still in elementary school.

George Putnam had been Harvard's treasurer for less than a year when he hired George Siguler. Over the objections of Putnam's predecessor, George Bennett, who through the aegis of State Street Research and Management Company was still managing the university's portfolio in 1973–74, Siguler had already engaged Harvard in a new investment technique called security lending. One of many "games" the management company perfected, security lending would for a time become so profitable for Harvard that it earned the sobriquet of a license to print money.

Across the River

FROM A COMPENSATION STANDPOINT, according to one of the university's consultants, Harvard for some people is a "fat tit." Bing Sung, a trader at Harvard Management Company, made $83,000 in fiscal 1981, while the president of the management company, Walter Cabot, made $140,000. Three years later, Cabot's base salary had risen to $195,000, and Sung's to $150,000. These figures were exclusive of fringe benefits including pension and, in the case of some people, low-interest loans for amounts as high as $200,000. In addition, key people participated in the company's deferred compensation plan, in which an additional 25 percent of their base salary was put into a pool, from which they could draw after their employment was terminated. In fiscal 1983, the company added over half a million dollars to this pool. Finally, some people received bonuses. By contrast, the highest academic salary at Harvard in 1983–84 was $129,000 for the dean of the Medical School, while the average full professor in the Faculty of Arts and Sciences earns about $55,000.

Salary increases at the management company, Siguler said,

were often 20 percent. He believes Walter Cabot, whose office was next to his, may make "half a million, with the perks," and that Bing Sung "is maybe the highest-paid in a given year."

Harvard is sensitive about this for two reasons. Though the management company salaries are set to be competitive with those paid in the investment business, they are completely out of scale with the academic salaries Harvard pays. They are also extraordinarily high for people working for a nonprofit institution. And Harvard, like other nonprofit institutions, wants to protect that status.

Laws governing nonprofit institutions are explicit. "They must derive their income passively — from dividends, royalties, and so on," points out George Siguler. "But nonprofits can clearly have for-profit subsidiaries. MATEP was to have been that." On the other hand, "Harvard pays income taxes on the revenues associated with the *Harvard Business School Review* ads." One of the major questions raised about Harvard's security lending when that program began was whether money made from such lending was taxable.

Harvard estimates that the cost of running the management company is about one-third what the cost of outside management would be. Harvard is not alone among schools that manage their endowments internally. The endowments at the University of Chicago, Northwestern University, Cornell University, and the University of California are all so managed. In addition, Columbia University does so partially, as do the University of Texas and the University of Rochester. Harvard made a decision after the Harvard Management Company was set up not to manage the investments of any other institution, though it has received many requests to do so. Such a policy would contradict Harvard's intent in having a company that gives its full attention to Harvard, and, again, legal questions regarding the company's not-for-profit status might be raised.

Harvard's annual reports of the treasurer to the Board of Overseers chronicle the official history of the Harvard Management Company. In the 1972–73 report, George Putnam's first as treasurer, no mention of the still unformed company is made, but there is a note about the establishment of the first pooled income fund. The following year, Putnam included a special section in his report on "the reorganization of the treasurer's office." The establishment and initial staffing of the management company is summarized, and Putnam noted that in the early fall of 1973 (before the company had even moved into its 70 Federal Street offices and almost a year before the company began formal operation) Harvard had started lending securities. "With the institution of careful controls," Putnam wrote, "this practice has produced meaningful incremental income with very little increased risk."

During the next two years, the treasurer's report continued to carry a special section, now labeled as a report from the management company. Not until 1976–77 was the heading for this section simply "Report of the Harvard Management Company," and the next year the present Annual Report heading was finally adopted.

The reports highlight significant developments in the management of Harvard's endowment and provide a revealing window on many aspects of Harvard's financial affairs. For example, in the 1974–75 report, Harvard's General Investments Account, the reader learns, "represents virtually all the assets of the University, except for plant and equipment, and it is uniquely structured so that the receipts and disbursements of all University cash flows pass through the single endowment fund, thus minimizing operating balances and liquidity reserves." The following year, we read, "each member of the Harvard [Management Company] team is a 'partner,' not in the legal sense but because each individual shares in every step of the investment process." And, "The process of analyzing and measuring relative risk adjusted between stocks, bonds and short-term investments and the need to develop appropriate diversification schedules within the bond and equity portfolios have forced us to focus on such broad issues as worldwide economic, political and sociological trends. . . . We have been significantly assisted in this area by the Harvard faculty, who have provided knowledge and perspective on many broad issues so important to forming investment strategy." And, "We have also received valuable assistance from the Harvard Center for Research in Computing Technology in designing one of the more advanced information and control systems."

The 1976–77 report is very short, only one page, but it closes with a frank admission: "Because Harvard is willing and able to take the long term view, we hope to be able to capitalize on opportunities caused by distressed markets for above average returns." Options trading gets some ink in the next report, as does the use of arbitrage, and special note is made of what were then three pooled income funds and "numerous" charitable remainder trusts, annuity trusts, and unitrusts. "Harvard," the report states, "has, in effect, built a small and efficient trust department. . . . These activities reflect a true marriage between the goals of the donor, professional asset management and the accumulation of long-term assets for the University." Following a general summary of the company's first five years in the 1978–79 report, and more specific analyses in 1979–80 and 1980–81, followed again by general summary in 1981–82, the report toots its horn with a flourish in 1982–83. "The . . . commitment to higher risk levels was rewarded as Harvard's portfolios participated in the subsequent stock and bond rallies. The general investment pool grew by approximately $740 million during the fiscal year, for a total return, including income, of 42%. Income alone amounted to approximately $150 million, almost matching the 1982 total."

For the first time, the report that year included performance charts for return per general investment unit, for general investment income, and equity portfolio allocation, among others. "The Management Company has changed its operating structure during the past year," the report concluded, with the most important changes being in the decentralization of the decision-making responsibility. In January 1983, we restructured responsibilities to a series of smaller portfolios, each managed by a specified Management Company portfolio manager. We believe this strategy will enhance decision-making flexibility, develop the next generation of portfolio managers, and diversify our management style.

We have also continued to expand the use of financial futures. These instruments are used for a variety of strategies and enable the Management Company to adjust market exposure in a manner which is less expensive and allows for more market liquidity than the purchase or sale of the underlying investments. This expansion has also enabled further extension of our yield enhancement and hedge programs.

Another major program has been the upgrading of our automated portfolio accounting and reporting systems. At the present time, all major portfolio activity is automated and an analysis program using personal computers is well under way.

Spectacular as the 1982–83 return on Harvard's general endowment fund was, the average total return for the endowments of all colleges and universities that year was over 41 percent, according to the National Association of College and University Business Officers (NACUBO). At the end of that year, the nearly $2.5 billion market value of Harvard's endowment was about $122 million more than the second place University of Texas system. Princeton at about $1.25 billion was in third place, Yale at just over $1 billion was fourth, and Stanford, with an endowment of about $862 million, completed the top five. Fifty-three of the institutions reporting figures to NACUBO listed an endowment market value of more than $100 million.

Harvard's endowment on June 30, 1984, was still about $2.5 billion, with second place University of Texas at about $2.25 billion. Princeton was still third, up slightly in its total from the year before, and Yale fourth at slightly less than its last annual total. The University of Chicago was tenth at $517 million. Amherst College, with one of the highest endowments per student, was in forty-second place, at $132 million. The average return on endowments reporting to NACUBO in 1983–84 was minus 2.25 percent, a far cry from the year before.

Harvard's general investment holdings as of June 29, 1984, included $884 million in equities, of which nearly $600 million worth was nonindexed and the balance in an indexed fund. The largest equity holding was in IBM: a nearly $24.5 million market value was listed for 231,400 shares. The smallest equity holding was in the Dicomed Corporation: twenty-two hundred shares with a market value of $26,000. Harvard had about $250 million in direct investments and over $540 million in fixed-income securities. Income in 1983–84 from special investments, which include life income and charitable remainder trusts and pooled income funds, was over $8 million on a market value total of nearly $63 million.

The treasurer's report for that year reviews the decade.

The organization began with a nine-member investment group, which structured an overall investment philosophy necessary to attain the mandated returns on Harvard's $1.2 billion of general investment assets.

The General Investment Account has since grown by 110% to $2.5 billion. The Management Company has been a leader, breaking new ground in many previously untested and profitable investment areas including stock and bond loans, options, financial futures, bond and stock arbitrage, real estate, venture capital, leverage buyouts, risk arbitrage, indexed portfolios, and a variety of new fixed-income instruments. The growth of the endowment and the continuing diversification and integration of the financial markets required that the Management Company expand its staff and change its mode of operation. The Company has grown from the original group of nine to almost one hundred professionals and staff.

The growth of the organization and the complexity of the financial markets necessitated a management structure that provided for investment decision making at both the macro and micro levels. Consequently, separate pools of capital have been established with specific objectives. These pools are the responsibility of individuals inside the organization, supported by a team of analysts or professional investment managers employed by the Management Company. The results of these pools of capital are monitored closely and evaluated often to ensure that the prescribed objectives are being met. The allocation of the capital pools is performed by a committee of top management personnel. Daily and monthly meetings of investment professionals to exchange ideas and financial data support the investment decisions of the Company. In addition, the constant information flow from Wall Street and other investment professionals and experts augments the internal decision making. This management structure provides the creativity and flexibility required in today's rapidly changing, complex investment environment.

The growth and diversification of investments in the General Investment Account had to be coordinated with the upgrade of the Company's operational and control functions. Over the last two years the Management Company has installed computer systems that track daily all positions by investment strategy at market value. The systems also track the location of each security and the use of the position. The profit or loss in each of these securities is monitored and reported to the appropriate level of management on a timely basis.

The Management Company has expanded its services to the University to include the investment management of several pooled funds and the University's pension plan assets, as well as the efficient disposition of nonmarketable gifts and bequests. . . .

The significant increase in the volatility of both the equity and bond markets in recent years has added new challenge to the management of endowment assets. The Management Company has invested heavily, and we believe appropriately, in professionals who can bring to these challenging markets a creative approach. Our goals for the future remain the same as in the past — to preserve in real terms the value to the University of gifts it receives and to provide an increase in income to the schools that will counter the inflationary pressure on their level of expenses.

Several miles south of Boston, in a modern office complex owned by State Street Bank in the town of Quincy, James Meketa had just returned from a company outing in Nantucket. State Street Bank is the custodian of Harvard's money, and Meketa's office is provided rent free. Meketa owed a large part of his business success to Harvard. But Harvard, in the person of George Putnam and the form of the Harvard Management Company, was indebted to Meketa. As George Putnam prepared to resume his business career on a full-time basis, and the Harvard Campaign moved toward its conclusion, Meketa recalled vividly the heady days in the mid-1970s, when the campaign had not yet been announced but the Harvard Management Company was already thriving.

Meketa owns his company, James Meketa Associates, with his wife. He estimates its worth, were he to sell it, at $1 million to $1.5 million. He has three children, who attend the Shady Hill School in Cambridge. That costs him $15,000, which means he needs a before-tax income of $30,000 just to pay for his kids' education. One of his hobbies is astronomy, and he occasionally travels to western Massachusetts, where he goes to an observatory in the town of Northfield.

Meketa majored in physics as a Harvard undergraduate. While a student, he became active in Harvard Student Agencies, a student-run group of businesses. Upon his graduation in 1969, he went to work for a private company, National Information Services, where he was director of computer programming. "I was a naive twenty-two-year-old," he says. One of his first clients was a small bank, for which he did contract programming in a spin-off from National Information Services called TLM Systems Associates. Meketa quickly "saw the power of automation in banks and what a package of software could mean to banking automation." There was, however, "a problem" with this particular bank: "It went bankrupt!" TLM was a major creditor of the bank; it had just sold $100,000 worth of software to it. Looking back, Meketa says, "I discovered there were many dishonest people in the world." He also discovered there was "a lack of sophistication in financial markets." He was able to liquidate his company without declaring bankruptcy. Partners resurrected it as Saddlebrook, but Meketa was no longer part of it.

A few years out of college, Meketa worked for a while for a

Route 128 company, Interactive Data Corporation (IDC). Harvard, represented by Walter Cabot and George Siguler, came to that company and asked for help in automating a large in-house investment manager. IDC, Meketa says, "was the only company that offered creditable, large-scale economic data." A few months later, Meketa was the associate director of the Harvard Computer Center, and, remembering him from IDC, Siguler asked to "buy" one-fifth of Meketa's time for the Harvard Management Company.

"Not many people saw what was going on. George said Harvard should assess all assets by virtue of how they function in this brave new world. There was enormous entrenched disagreement, but gradually Siguler's views prevailed. Finance to George is not simply investing. It's a dynamic, active enterprise with dollars flowing constantly. George was street-smart and deep. He acquired a halo. He was a superstar." It pleased Meketa to say this; remembering his own association with Siguler, Meketa became increasingly animated, for it was his own story as well that he was telling.

As a nonprofit, Harvard enjoys certain investment advantages. It pays no tax on capital gains, short term or long. Siguler, says Meketa, "wanted to use that benefit. But to do so, he needed to keep close control of the endowment." The endowment "had to be managed closely," because this "was a fast-paced, aggressive game. Most old concepts were not true. Siguler wanted to quantify success."

One of the first things the Harvard Management Company did was bring all the endowment together in one giant "pool." Though the bulk of this super-fund was to be managed internally, initially five outside managers managed 5 to 8 percent of the endowment, "to create," the company said in its first annual report, "a healthy diversification." Harvard could not rely on only certain strategies. And there was a need for a way to measure what it did. State Street Bank had agreed in contract to provide such a service, but the bank didn't have that capability.

"I was the only person who knew how to do this," says Meketa. The bank asked Harvard to hire Meketa as a consultant, and Meketa formed a company to teach the bank how to provide the service. For the next eight or so years, Meketa "was a major conduit between the bank and Harvard."

To begin, he laid out for the bank what it needed to do. Meketa "assumed everything could be measured somehow." He had "a naive notion that this was much simpler than physics," but he discovered the bank's math then was "pre-Newton in some cases." State Street "was already very good at collecting data," and Meketa built the software the bank needed to measure endowment performance.

One of Siguler's most important ideas was to leverage some of Harvard's largest holdings through the practice of security lending. To leverage an asset means to use it as the basis for acquiring another asset. A person who owns a house, borrows money against it, and uses the borrowed money to buy a second house that he then sells at a profit is leveraging his original asset.

Say Harvard owned $60 million worth of IBM stock. Siguler assumed Harvard would own that stock a long time. Why not leverage it? No one had thought of doing this before with a private university's securities. It smacked of overt profit making.

Imagine a broker who suddenly needed $60 million worth of IBM stock to deliver to a buyer. If his brokerage house doesn't have the stock in its own inventory, or if the brokerage house's record-keeping department is behind, it may be cheaper for the broker to borrow the stock so he can deliver it immediately and be paid. For the lender — Harvard — this becomes a way of doing something more with the stock than holding on to it, earning dividends from it, and hoping for an increase in value.

Siguler made certain that Harvard was fully collateralized when it lent stock. Harvard demanded and received 105 percent collateral in the form of cash and treasury bills. Harvard then earned further money on the collateral, all the while retaining the ownership, including dividends, of the stock it had lent. Harvard shared its profit from the collateral fifty-fifty with the broker.

Harvard's half of this profit was at no risk — a license to print money! Soon, Harvard was lending $1 million a month; within one year, about 30 percent of the stocks lent worldwide were from the Harvard Management Company.

Security lending was a daily business with much paperwork. It swamped State Street's computers, creating a major administrative problem. Further automation was needed, which Harvard had to get on its own. Assistant Treasurer Henry Ameral kept separate books to stay on top of this. Only once did a brokerage that had borrowed securities from Harvard go bankrupt. Because Harvard was always 105 percent collateralized, the major risk of getting involved with a weak brokerage firm was the poor public relations that could result. Had this happened a lot, it would have hurt Harvard's image. Another "fear," as Ameral called it, was that Harvard would not have time to convert a letter of credit (for the collateral) to cash. If there were a default, Ameral said, "we would have run like hell to the bank that issued the letter."

George Putnam was not a man to let such things bog him, or Harvard, down. Harvard's independent treasurer, who drove a Chevy Cavalier when he could have afforded a chauffeured limousine, who owned waterfront property in Manchester and Maine worth millions but worried over an eight-dollar electric bill, didn't see an anomaly in the management company's work. In his eyes, the results mattered, not the methods. Making money for Harvard was the company's goal, whether in stock lending or more traditional investments. He gave his blessing to security lending, and when someone else on the Harvard Corporation asked him for details he brought Siguler along with him to explain. Some of those questions came from Derek Bok, who also served on the management company's board of directors, but Bok had essentially signed off on the company's course when he approved its formation. He had too many other concerns, and he didn't understand what the management company was engaged in. Neither, in some ways, did Putnam. But Siguler did.

"George [Siguler] invented a new service, and ruthlessly exploited it," says Meketa. "He believed traditional notions of value in investing were flawed. . . . It was not always intellectuals who were involved. They believed in the old notions of bonds being safe, equities speculative. George said, 'That's bullshit.' He said bonds are just as risky, they're just an IOU."

Meketa's consulting business was growing and was incorporated in 1978. He "saw an opportunity to build tools for a new human enterprise: was it really possible to manage money rationally?" He began to separate himself from Harvard, gradually taking on more consulting, and his Harvard role became smaller as his own business grew. George Siguler was impatient. He soon viewed security lending as old hat; pension funds had discovered it, and with more players in the game, it wasn't as profitable. "Boring," he called it. There were more new worlds to conquer, and he needed people other than Jim Meketa to help him do it.

Bing Sung operated on what he called four modes. His normal mode was bearish; his second mode was more bearish. His "good mode" was neutral, and feeling ebullient he was "reluctantly bullish." Today, he was "a cautious bull in the market. If the market weakens," he said, "I'm going to have to take some defensive measures. I'm long. I'm a very nervous bull."

Sung usually arrived at the Harvard Management Company from his home in Andover, Massachusetts, around 7:30 A.M. Harvard '66, with a Harvard Ph.D. in statistics earned at the age of twenty-three in 1970, Sung taught for several years at the Harvard Business School, where one of his students was George Siguler. It was Siguler who later hired him to work at the management company, after Sung had gained experience and begun to make a reputation for himself on Wall Street as, according to Jim Meketa, "an options trading wizard." Sung dressed differently from most of his colleagues. Instead of the suits that the other men and women wore, he was typically attired in corduroy pants and V-neck sweater. And he spoke to his colleagues in terms not usually associated with the world of high-stakes finance. During periods of peak trading pressure, when he was simultaneously watching a video display of option prices and carrying on a telephone conversation, his favorite nickname for fellow traders was "Sweetie."

To be a trader, you have to understand the market, know something about banking, know a lot about many different companies, have a solid grasp of sophisticated economics and mathematics, and be a good judge of people. It also helps to be smart. Sung's IQ was once tested at 169.

Options trading is one of the oldest forms of commercial activity. Rather than buying or selling a commodity, security, or property, a person buys or sells the *right* to make a purchase or sale at a later, prearranged date. To do this, the buyer of an option pays a premium, or fee, that is not recoverable. An option to buy is a call, and an option to sell is a put. When the agreed-on date for a call or put is reached, the holder of the option has the right to exercise his option. He may forgo that right, but in any case he loses the premium he paid earlier, as well as what he might have earned by investing that premium differently.

In the trading world of Bing Sung, buying and selling puts and calls has been raised to an art form made possible by computer technology. Using highly sophisticated financial information that would be unavailable without the aid of computers, option traders engage in a seemingly infinite number of put-and-call strategies — for example, buying puts and callls on, say, the same bond. This is called risk hedging. Split-second decision making is often necessary, since theoretically any new piece of information will eventually be known by everyone playing the market, and the market will respond accordingly. Thus, a trader must react very quickly when something "moves," since his profit rests on beating the rest of the market. It is not surprising that traders often burn out by the age of forty, unable to cope further with the tension that this form of investment creates.

In charge of Harvard's equity-related trading and the "very treacherous" area of bond options and bond futures, Sung talks about his work in a rush, the words tumbling out. "There's a tremendous amount of latitude, within guidelines," he says. "It seems too good to be true. I have to pinch myself. Our basic rule — and I have to hand it to Walter — is we're willing to try anything, but it: one, has to be legal; two, has to be controllable, that is, measurable; three, has to make some intuitive sense of why Harvard, a nonprofit, should have an edge; and four, has to make money."

By 8:45 A.M., Sung goes on to "automatic pilot," and doesn't go off it until around 4:15 P.M. In the extraordinarily existential day of the traders, multi-million-dollar decisions are made rapidly and repeatedly, and there are usually multiple conversations being carried on.

"Hewlett opened at thirty-five and five eighths," trader Jeff Smith says.

"There's a dividend stream on the eighty-five," another voice calls, referring to something on his video screen.

Investment policy chief Nils Peterson stops by at the trading desk. "Since Walter's extremely bullish on the markets," Sung says to him, "I don't want to touch his longs."

"We'll cover this Hewlett at five or better," Smith says, to no one in particular.

The comments, in an atmosphere of controlled tension, are continuous, all made in a language peculiar to the profession. No one sits around with nothing to do. The management of Harvard's investments takes place against a backdrop of daily drama. By three o'clock one afternoon, the face of a trader for the Harvard Management Company shows dried sweat, and there is a sheen of dried sweat on his hair. The phone banks before each trader have ninety-six buttons, most marked in a shorthand — "In," "WATS," "Sol Bost," "Merr Lynch" — that identifies the line or the party at the other end of the direct connection. Bing Sung has just processed a large pile of mail, most of which he has put in the wastebasket. On average, he looks at each piece less than ten seconds.

"Bondinoes!" Jeff Smith exclaims.

"Spot sixty!" another voice hollers.

Sung picks up his phone. "Trader," he snaps. "Our over-the-counter expert?" he continues, smiling.

"Spots down four."

"Davey, what do you hear on money supplies?"

"Big volume in Sterling today."

"Jeff, you overbought your Delta calls."

"Nice sweater, Liz."

"Sweetie!"

"He's crazy."

"Holy shit, look at Phelps Dodge!"

Jeff Smith takes a call from Philadelphia and shouts over to Bing Sung. "Miami's down four and a half," he says, referring to the point spread in a football game. Sung immediately picks up his phone while Smith is still delivering his message.

"Hello?" Sung says. And then, "Yeah, I know." A pause. Another "yeah." From the look on his face, he's received some bad news affecting a bet he's made on the game.

"Uh-huh. I know, I know. But this is *my* money we're talking about here."

Sung's reputation is national. In 1985, he was the subject of features in two national investment magazines. "These articles," he said, "should be of very little interest to anyone, except possibly my parents." In fact, they were of very great interest to many people, including the vast majority of investment managers who cannot duplicate what Sung does with "enhanced-index arbitrage" and "selling winged straddles." Sung worked at the developing edge of his profession. He was a performer. What he did each day was monitored, but no one could do it for him. Nerve-racking, creative, and taxing, trading is a lonely art.

When a brokerage house executes a contract, Sung said, it costs them one dollar. The Harvard Management Company, because it is not on the trading floor, has to pay $15 for each such execution. Yes, Sung continued, "Harvard had looked into opening its own firm. But there was too much overhead. It's better to pay the commissions." There were disadvantages. Buying conversions — a certain combination of stocks, puts, and calls: "Only the sharpest [brokerages] still have running. And possibly S&P futures and options may become like that." Meketa explained later that "games gradually get squeezed. All these things have little increments such that, at some point, they become losing games." The talk was detailed and complicated. There was nothing, apparently, the management company hadn't looked into. Even underwriting, acting as an investment bank, even that the company had investigated. There was a lot of "complicated stuff." When Harvard sold a bond issue, the management company was "floating the debt for a second, they were buying from us.

"The only difference," Sung continued, "between most investment speculation and a bet is the time you hold the paper. All we do is use the underlying assets for collateral. It's not like the marketing–idea–production areas at GM that interlock." There were now about a dozen equity trading accounts at the management company. Four managers oversaw a variety of portfolios, to give the company's investments the mix necessary to balance risk and reward. The "games" were then making about $1 million a month. Sung thought they were capable of doing thirty million a year. Even in a bad year, he says, they ought to be able to make enough to fund the entire budget of the management company.

Sung was thirty-eight, and that age is nearing senior citizen status for a trader. In another five to seven years, he thought, it would be surprising to him if he were still doing the same work. For the first time in his professional life, he could imagine getting up in the morning and not going in to trade. He had come back recently from a vacation, but by his own admission, "wasn't invigorated.

"What distinguishes winners from losers? We are like a casino, because we have deep pockets and patience. We can weather the storm." He was talking about Harvard now; not every trader could say this. His voice was now completely animated. "I love it. It's like a poker game, every day a new hand. Christ, every minute sometimes."

Increasingly, he operated independently. For more than a year the traders had not based their decisions on Harvard's equity holdings. Before, there had been much more formal coordination, and options were "tied into the rest of the portfolio," in what Sung called "group investment decisions." Now they were "uncoupled, untracked, cut free." Like "every tub on its own bottom" in Cambridge, "every portfolio was on its own." Sung could buy an option whether or not Harvard owned the underlying stock. "In the old days," he said, "if the portfolio didn't like chemicals, I wouldn't. Now, I might buy puts. There's a lot less integrating."

There was a time in the investment world when the question, Siguler says, was : "Do we buy IBM at one-twenty, yes or no? It was an on/off light switch. Now it's a galaxy. People who didn't see this . . ." Siguler shook his head. Clearly, Bing Sung was not one of those people. Sung understood there was money to be made in the exploitation of investment strategies that had to do with more than the dividend a company paid. Investment here turned on the market's perception rather than a company's production.

Siguler's name inspired a strong reaction. Siguler was one of Bing Sung's first students at the Harvard Business School. He was "very bright, but he winged it," says Sung, meaning Siguler's comprehension of a point's general importance was often greater than his grasp of its specific details. Sung left teaching because he "was more interested in making money than in writing stuff that no one would read."

Siguler was "arguably the moving force for certain things," said Sung, "but he never did anything without Walter's approval." Walter Cabot was not a figurehead. Still, Siguler had been a kind of "assistant to the chairman of the board," who was George Putnam. "He was the clerk at all the board of directors' meetings. But he wasn't the president. He was outside the regular hierarchy. Only in his last year was he finally given the title of associate treasurer.

"With George, there's no bullshit. He sees through the fucking bullshit. He doesn't hide, he's not afraid. He has twenty-twenty hindsight, forgets his mistakes. But he makes very few."

Sung compared the management company to a ship, on which Siguler served "kind of two and a half functions. He ran the operations, he was first mate. He was indirectly the chief engineer, of trading. Research and equity — the galley — he left to others, but he took charge of the bedroom area — venture capital, special activities. In other words, he left the galley alone, though he sat in on meetings, but more as an equal participant than an overseer."

Talking about Siguler and Cabot and Putnam, Sung said, was "like talking to six blind men and an elephant.

"How often did those three men meet as a trio?" Sung asked rhetorically. "How often was Putnam the referee? There was not terribly much three-way conversation."

Walter Cabot took his M.B.A. at Harvard Business School in 1959, and after seven years with Putnam Management Company became senior investment officer and managing director of Wellington Management Company, Inc. Cabot's uncle, Paul Cabot, once held Putnam's position as Harvard treasurer. Paul Cabot was a man who did things his own way. Prudent and profane, he kept some of the university's investment earnings hidden, so he could miraculously produce emergency funds when needed, and he loved to tell off-color jokes. He bowed to no one. The first time he saw John F. Kennedy after Kennedy's election as president, Paul Cabot said to Kennedy, who was then a Harvard overseer, "How's the new job, Jack?"

His nephew, while less the extrovert, possessed an equally

shrewd, equally practical mind. He was a gentleman in a business where manners didn't make money. Many years before, Cabot was the first man Putnam had taken under his wing, though Cabot didn't like to think of it that way, since he was only a few years younger than Putnam. Siguler had been the last.

Cabot was forty years old when he accepted the job as president of the newly formed Harvard Management Company, and he soon put together a staff of senior investment professionals, all of whom were older than George Siguler. The difference in ages didn't faze Siguler in the least. "My youth has always been a disadvantage," he would say ten years later, as though he were unaware that he sounded immodest.

Cabot's sedate sixth-floor corner office is located directly underneath Bing Sung's high-tech bailiwick on the seventh. Sometimes Cabot meets people in the board room, just down the hallway, with its large table and oriental rug. Around a corner from this room is the receptionist's area, where an oil portrait of his uncle faces a wall decorated with a Harvard Veritas shield. An exceedingly polite man, who despite a limp still walks visitors to the elevator when they leave, Cabot is Harvard's dodge-ball coach extraordinaire. He contends with the conflict of egos that is inevitable in an organization employing a trader as talented and certain of his ability as Bing Sung. For ten years, he had to balance the benefit of Siguler's ideas with the deficit of his, Cabot's, undermined authority. He had to please Putnam, mollify Siguler, and set the right tone for the rest of his staff, which needed to know he was in charge. And, as the company grew, as it moved into such new areas as venture capital, he had to juggle his loyalty to Harvard with his business judgment when people approached him on business.

"A lot of people out there who are alumni would like to stick a knife in your gut if it is of benefit to them. There are a lot of unscrupulous alumni with 'great deals.' You can get into a lot of hot water. Some are honest misinterpretations. And obviously you have to be diplomatic. The guys you know are trying to skin you you try to avoid. It's always difficult to say no, except to the guy who's a real bastard. You have to be a little cute, a little sensitive. You have to accommodate the honest donors. But you aren't going to put up with the others.

"Harvard is Harvard. It's also Mr. Deep Pocket. You must try to avoid the land mines. Harvard is carefully watched. It's a big account. There is a tendency for some to think that if Harvard does something it must be good. That's bullshit."

Cabot's accent is a mix of Boston and WASP. His hair is usually slightly askew, and he pushes it frequently with his hands as he talks. He wears horn-rimmed glasses.

There are a number of issues when someone gives money to Harvard, Cabot said. Harvard "has the opportunity to manage it. The donor takes the characteristic deduction. Harvard is not the fiduciary manager." There are life income funds, pooled income funds, lead trusts. Both the donor and Harvard benefit, Cabot said. The donor "gets the benefit of Harvard Management Company for free." The company manages about 150 trusts, and Cabot said he has spoken personally with twenty to twenty-five of the donors.

"Say a donor comes in, just him and his wife, sixty-five years old, and at the end of his life wants to give everything to Harvard, but now only wants to give twenty percent. Will Harvard help him with the other eighty percent?" Cabot asked rhetorically. "We're not set up to manage individual portfolios. And there are legal questions," he continued.

"The Harvard Management Company is a first-class investment organization, willing to pay people and to have incentive programs." But the managers there "have traded the entrepreneurial reward for the job satisfaction of working in such an enterprise." Cabot added that he "has to keep this an exciting place to work."

The company's board of directors is made up of the president of Harvard, the treasurer (who is chairman), and seven others, including Robert Stone. "Bok claims he doesn't know much about investments," Cabot said, "but he's interested in the process. He doesn't interfere. He exercises his fiduciary responsibility, which he should. He's available to me. He's chairman of the board of the executive committee [of Harvard]. He sets a good tone for us.

"I don't necessarily agree this is a young man's business. It's also a business of experience and judgment and perspective." Cabot said he "tries to be useful. Harvard has done a hell of a good job for three hundred and fifty years, I'd like to go for twenty. But I don't have tenure."

Harvard's "is a high visibility account," Cabot continued. The company is "not trying to promote a business." It "has to satisfy the boss. But facts stand on their own." The background is "generally conservative. There is a sense of values. You make some mistakes but you hope you're then better at dealing with them."

Sometimes the tension got to Cabot. In early 1982, after Bing Sung had been at the company three years, he remembers "Siggy and Cabot screaming at each other. They were shouting 'Fuck you' at each other." Sung called George Putnam, the only time he'd ever done so, and asked to meet with him.

"Putnam gave me a lot of time, about forty-five minutes to an hour. He'd told Cabot that I was going to see him, and Walter asked me the next day, 'Did the roof explode?'" Fearing that Cabot was inquiring about the purpose of Sung's visit with Putnam, Sung instead learned from Cabot that the president of Putnam Management Company had resigned the day Sung had been talking with Putnam. "Putnam never let on. That impressed me. My problem seemed a tempest in a teapot." There was, Sung adds, "no more shouting." Ever the smooth politician, Siguler would later insist there had been no shouting.

The company's sixth-floor library includes in its collection many annual reports, among them its own. The company uses another full floor, plus two half floors, of the building at 70 Federal Street. A device called a Quotron and electronic tickers for Standard and Poor's 500 and the Dow Jones averages are prominently on view. Video display terminals for the company's own computer system are on desks everywhere. The carpet is light blue, and there are large windows in all the outer offices, with more glass on the interior walls of the corner offices. The furnishings are modern.

The bond portfolio analysts are on the seventh floor. The area around one corner office is spacious, and there are reports all about. Nearby is the cash desk, where transactions are handled; the actual trades are made through brokerage houses. Several equity portfolio analysts work with the portfolio managers, and their desks are located along spaces like corridors which connect one section of a floor with another. In one corner is the stock loan and bond desk.

Quarters are close at the trading desk. Beyond, there is space before the next desks. Because of all the video display terminals and other equipment and reference materials on top of the trading desks, you can't see over them to the next area. In the corner at one end of the inverse horseshoe of trading desks is a framed certificate, dated March 3, 1982, for 1,727,340 shares of a company Harvard received in a bequest.

Two floors down, in far less conspicuous quarters, Henry Ameral heads the gifts and trusts department behind a door marked only with a small plaque. Visitors to the management company come and go with little notice, rarely questioned by anyone other than the receptionist about their reasons for being in the building. Ameral, who began working for Harvard when Paul Cabot was still treasurer, remembers a day "when people used to walk in off the street to make their gifts. Years ago, the busiest time in Boston was from ten-thirty A.M. until twelve-thirty P.M., when the brokers' windows were open to deliver securities."

There were about a dozen equity trading accounts at the management company in early 1985. The four portfolio managers oversaw a Standard and Poor–type index portfolio, a straight equity account, a value account, and the pooled and special funds.

The Harvard Management Company's performance reviews and measurement instruments grew in sophistication. Initially, they were not unlike those Jim Meketa developed for the State Street Bank and Trust Company. A portfolio manager's returns, for example, could be summarized and compared to that of other managers and to Standard and Poor's 500 or ninety-day treasury bills. The manager's portfolio could be broken down and the rate of return for each component measured over time. A vast array of numbers could be generated, showing fluctuations in that rate month by month — even, as the techniques used by the management company were refined, day by day. Moreover, detailed reports of equity characteristics and bond characteristics could be prepared, showing such things as the "maturity, coupon, quality and sector distribution of a portfolio," with indexes weighted by market values.

The schedule of meetings at the Harvard Management Company during one typical month included four sessions on research priorities, one strategy meeting, a discussion of industry spreadsheets, something called "Skeleton Day," and four different presentations by representatives of outside firms. For example, a money market economist from Goldman Sachs spoke one morning.

The management company's operations are discussed in at least every other meeting of the Harvard Corporation. Endowment questions, says Corporation member Andrew Heiskell, "are always a misery.

"Equity markets behaved very badly in the past few years. If they hadn't, we wouldn't have had to increase tuition so much. The endowment was not keeping pace with the consumer price index.

"The management company is now one of the most risk-hedged operations. It simply can't be down ten percent when everyone else is up ten percent, because there is a psychological factor as well as dollars and cents."

People work at the Harvard Management Company, operations chief Donald Beane said, because "there is a tremendous amount of capital and freedom. It boils down to varying degrees of these sorts. That's what makes it fun — a lot of money to play with. I shouldn't say that. And an environment that allows freedom to look for the new."

Beane, whose duties include supervising Bing Sung and the other traders, has worked for the management company since 1981. Before that, he was at Morgan Stanley in New York. He is a graduate of Lehigh University, and he went to Columbia Business School, where he finished in 1969. He worked for Olin and then TWA before joining Morgan Stanley. He was treasurer there before he left and did planning and financial analysis.

A "head hunter dug" Beane up, he said. Beane's "claim to fame was systems, management control, a knowledge of the trading world and accounting." In Beane's view, the management company has now gone "from the brass age to the late 1970s." It shouldn't be called a pioneer, he insisted. On the contrary, "we're laggards." Beane wears gold-rimmed glasses and his hair is black. On his desk were cassette tapes of Billy Joel, Kenny Rogers, and Barbra Streisand.

There are about forty people in operations and control, and Beane manages them. And he spends a lot of his time trading. He called himself "a risk cop for the whole place." He must understand what risks are being taken. There are different kinds of risks, such as how much out of stocks a portfolio manager can be.

The Harvard Management Company once had every security position on a card, said Beane. There was "a manual evaluation of ownership" for the basic portfolio. Operations "were no problem." Options "was the clearest type of example of the need for knowing where you stand each morning. The most difficult problem for me was training the organization and people here to go from one kind of world to another. And the business has to go on while you're introducing automation." The training and development of people "is more challenging than getting software."

The management company realized in mid-1980, he said, that "security control and operational analysis was chaotic. The controlled report capability was not being utilized. This is a common problem."

Beane said he "likes big things, likes to start from scratch." There was no commercially available software to do what he wanted to do. He spent a year planning. By late 1984, the transition was complete. But the work "never ends. The securities business is constant." The computer runs are now made every day, as they are with any large money manager.

There "is nothing unique because it's Harvard," Beane said, "other than the organization." Prior to the advent of portfolio managers, there was just one big portfolio. In late 1982 and early 1983, the portfolio was segmented, responsibility was delegated. Beane called it "a fund of funds that has one client." The number of funds varies between twelve and eighteen.

"Individuals are suddenly on line for their investment decisions." He used the word *accountability,* mentioned an increase in "the demand for information and accuracy in accounting. Measurement is pretty standard. But some of the stuff is tailor made. The portfolios are not industry-based. One guy does an index portfolio, another long-term."

He described the atmosphere as "extremely free." People are trusted, but "this requires a good control system. And it builds healthy competition. The tone and feel and touch of the organization is more important" than measurement. And the company is now "healthier than it was before. It's reasonably loose."

There is a monthly meeting of senior people. The research department has a continuing series of meetings with portfolio managers "to find out what analysts should be looking into. The analysts' group always focuses on a mix."

Beane on security lending and the use of arbitrage: "There the Harvard Management Company has been a pioneer. It was one of the first nonprofits, if not the first, to do. And it was one of the first to go into venture capital, and options."

The company does an in-house credit analysis of everyone

with whom it does business, with a set credit limit established. There has been one default, in the mid-seventies. Harvard had a loan out but it was covered with cash. The company is "reasonably prudent, it has reasonably tight limits." And it's collateralized in every transaction taken. "The spreads in the business are so thin now that it doesn't make sense to take an unnecessary risk," Beane continued.

"The Harvard Corporation has said, 'Manage the money with certain objectives,'" Beane explained. "There is a high degree of flexibility in the manner of how this is done. A high degree of public presence is sometimes good and sometimes bad. And partners here will never have ownership of the company. It's not a place for entrepreneurs, for someone who wants to totally control his own destiny." Beane used the term "psychic control." The company can't offer an individual that, he said.

The Harvard name was a factor in attracting people, but, "in a sense, who cares what the label is on the door? But, in another, here's the world's greatest university." Beane agreed this was a young man's business. At the age of forty, he was one of the oldest employees of the company.

In Cambridge one day to do some astronomy research, Jim Meketa said, "The whole business of finance is so machine-intensive now it's not appreciated." The investment decisions Bing Sung made "require seeing information before it works its way through the system." All that, Meketa said, was made possible by on-line computers, which may seem secondary, which may seem, in a sense, "a convenience" — but without which the modern investment world would "shut down."

Siguler admits that "if you disaggregate the components of the management company, you can see there's stuff that is nothing to write about." On the other hand, the relatively new area of venture capital "made a thirty-nine percent profit the year I left."

Siguler laughed, remembering the time he'd told Vice President and General Counsel Daniel Steiner, a serious, tight-lipped guardian of Harvard's reputation, that the management company was going to invest in a Playboy Club. He *thought* Steiner knew he was joking. But still, the memory of it, just the image of Steiner's nonplussed reaction, was amusing.

Using the analogy of a gambling casino, which may lose money some nights but comes out ahead on most, George Siguler talked about Harvard's investment advantage in many of the schemes he devised. "We were the house," Siguler said, talking about security lending. "We were never in a position where the odds were against us. Most passive institutional investors don't think of themselves as traders. There are institutional, comparative advantages they don't take advantage of."

What Siguler understood intuitively about Harvard's investments would, just a generation before, have been considered heresy. So profound was the change represented by this quiet revolution that it had taken place without a general cognizance of it even among Harvard's own administration.

"The cost of being Harvard," George Siguler said, "is uniquely high." Siguler illustrated his remark with his recollection of helping to write a statement on Harvard's investments in companies that do business in South Africa. "The first printing was seven thousand copies," he said, indicating with a raise of his moustache as he pronounced the first syllable of the word *thousand* that at any other school the number would have been far lower. "Harvard sets the national standard," he said. "It's an unparalleled national treasure."

It was the kind of remark you could not imagine George Putnam making, though not one with which he would take issue. Siguler made them often, as though he were still uncertain he was a Harvard man.

Investments, he continues, "is a business where the good people are always undercompensated and the average are overcompensated." Siguler, who clearly includes himself in the former category but hardly could be considered undercompensated, loves to talk like this, questioning what he sees as the arbitrary limits individuals and institutions impose on themselves. He believes fund-raising campaigns should be in "an almost continuous drive mode." And $350 million, Siguler thinks, was too low a goal for the Harvard Campaign. He thinks the goal should have been $500 million, because of Harvard's "broad base of wealth."

This, says Jim Meketa, "is not the Smith Barney way! Not all the players in the game can do this." Meketa felt that with so many people involved, "if someone screws up, it can cause a mess." And at the management company there was, he felt, no adequate hedge. He was concerned that so much of the Harvard endowment was now in "side games," while other forms of investment had been discredited.

"It's high tech, very sophisticated. Siguler saw Harvard's endowment as a large pool to be used as aggressively as possible." But Meketa sensed "social forces" at work: "Anything that's too good to be true gets away from you. You take it too far, overplay your hand. Egos get inflated. The house of cards collapses. You must accept from the beginning that you are shadow boxing."

Meketa's own business was going well, and he did little now for the management company, where Siguler's ghost hovered over the traders' desks. And not long before, a Boston banker, Roderick MacDougall, had quietly taken George Putnam's place as treasurer. Walter Cabot and Bing Sung wondered what changes lay ahead.

"It's a heavily macho-laden game," continued Meketa, "assuming that smart people can take part of the other guy's share of future growth. This is nonsense. It's a zero-sum game, in aggregate. Someone wins, but for every winner there is a loser."

Harvard, through its management company, was a "winner." The loser was harder to name. The small private investors, who hadn't the resources of the management company, who couldn't pay a Bing Sung to look out for them: they were losers. And taxpayers who couldn't claim exemption from capital gains: they were losers, too, of sorts. But these imprecise generalizations were hard to see, hard to calculate.

Putnam would return in June for at least one more Harvard commencement. Though it was still officially a secret, the Corporation, as was the usual custom, had voted him an honorary degree the year following his retirement.

Hugh Calkins, a lawyer from Cleveland who was the senior fellow, had just announced his resignation from the Corporation, effective the end of June. Putnam had received a letter about this today. The two-page typed single-spaced letter, on corporate stationery, was addressed "Dear George" and signed "Derek," and it invited Putnam to recommend a replacement for Calkins. Such recommendations were to be marked "*Confidential*" on the envelope in which they were enclosed, the letter said.

Putnam still liked to talk shop: "Options on the averages are more interesting than just options. For example, futures on the S and P five hundred. When the market changes rapidly, you can buy them much more quickly than the individual equities, then replace them as you buy the equities. Also, when you buy futures you put up ten percent. So you can put the other ninety percent in short government notes. You get the full benefit of the market but higher income than the stocks would bring in. The management company also uses very sophisticated bond immunization. You use bond futures to take the fluctuations out of the bond portfolio.

"Derek didn't like our doing things Princeton and Yale weren't. He never really understood some of 'the games.' "

Putnam carried his briefcase through the larger room beyond his office, stopped, and locked the large double lobby doors himself. He'd been in Hawaii recently, then Florida, "so we've had two goof-offs."

"Putnam was an informal investment leader," said Walter Cabot. " 'Where can I be helpful?' he would ask. He was less involved in neat and tidy process."

Siguler was supposed to have had lunch that day with Walter Cabot in Boston, and to visit with George Putnam, too, but he canceled his plans because he had the flu. Cabot, who sometimes referred to Siguler as "a bulldozer," said, "Siguler clearly loved rubbing elbows with the high and mighty. In his absence, we have filled in some slots, made ourselves more stable. George started lots of balls rolling. This company has become more structured rather than less. Yes, we used to get mad at each other. He would tell me I was wrong about something. But I never considered firing him."

"I pushed the place, pushed people, scared the hell out of some people," Siguler says. "But not in a malicious sense. I have a strong bias toward doing things."

Earlier, standing one evening at the corner of Franklin and Federal streets in downtown Boston, Walter Cabot — who had just left his office with its potted plant and papers and, on a low window shelf, paperback edition of David Halberstam's *The Best and the Brightest* — was on his way home on foot for a quick dinner, before traveling to Wellesley for a 7 P.M. meeting of the Wellesley College trustees, with whom he served as treasurer. "The management company was once *cozy*," he had said before. And then, commencing a minute before he looked at his watch and continuing as he put a few papers in his briefcase, got his overcoat, and walked to the elevator: "Do the forces of change come from within or without? No one knows the answer. Any organization has to have some boldness, some ability to take risks. Our machine is better run. . . . It's important not to stamp out that creativity. I just hired a new portfolio manager from Morgan Stanley. He wants to practice his art, his craft. One must always remember, the Harvards of the world would never have started without that creativity."

George Putnam, believed Assistant Treasurer Henry Ameral, "was the first to recognize" what lay ahead. "Regardless of what happens now, the structure will be there." Not everyone was so certain.

Taking care of the money Harvard already had and the new funds coming in, George Putnam — and Harvard — benefited from Putnam's relationship with George Siguler. Putnam, too busy to closely supervise the Harvard Management Company, installed Walter Cabot as president, but it was Siguler, operating outside the company's hierarchy, who used his relationship with Putnam to move Harvard into high-tech investment. Putnam needed someone to keep him informed. He was also, Cabot thought, "mesmerized" by Siguler. The old money of Manchester married the new from Cleveland, and soon Harvard was lending securities and employing an options trading genius. In 1985, pledging $50 million of Harvard's endowment, the management company was one of thirty-two investors proposing as a consortium organized by Morgan Stanley & Company to buy Conrail. But with these new ventures came new risks, and Harvard's new treasurer, Roderick MacDougall, devoting much more time to his work than Putnam had, focused on them. MacDougall's banking background would be especially important, for Harvard had made some financial decisions in the past decade that resulted in a huge debt — over $600 million. Important matters of policy, ranging from the receipt of federal research funds to the investment of Harvard money in companies that do business in South Africa, were intertwined with each other and with Harvard's overall finances. Everything was connected.

"The fear now," said Jim Meketa, "is that with the endowment's sophistication, the level of people required goes way up." Incompetence could be very costly. There was always the possibility that Harvard would forget, say, to cover an option position, and such mistakes could mean a loss in the millions. And as Harvard "does ever more complicated deals," Meketa explained, the size of such a mistake increases. But the real worry centered on "the bright, egotistical people" who were running the endowment. What if a trader "flipped out"? What if he made a mistake and then, to cover it, doubled his bet, believing in his own invulnerability?

"Harvard has gone from a DC-3, sturdy and reliable, to an incredibly powerful streamlined plane," continued Meketa. "It needs a perpetually humble pilot. So much is leveraged now.

There are tentacles reaching everywhere. Account controls are necessary. MacDougall can immunize some of this by being a nitpicker. But things in and of themselves don't prevent disasters. So the checkers of the checkers are now very powerful. Investments is still a game where your word is your bond. Harvard could now employ five Bing Sungs. But Harvard will always be vulnerable to a person's mistakes.

"This is as wide as society itself. The whole game is faster, more complicated, more sophisticated. And it's riskier. At Harvard, the risk is a little less, because you have more, smarter people, and fewer highly paid professionals. There are fewer financial risks that someone's going to take a flyer." It was unlikely, in other words, that Harvard would ever get itself into the kind of flagrant abuse of the system for personal gain as had several executives at E. F. Hutton. "But common sense has to tell you that anytime you're in a game in which big decisions must be made in a few seconds, there's no time for reflection."

The senior strategist for the management company, John Chase, spoke of "the relatively small, reasonably close-knit group" that comprised the company until about 1982 and of how it had become "much more departmentalized." George Siguler's former assistant, Michael Thonis, who had worked on the financing plans for MATEP and technology transfer, had now, as research director, overhauled the company's group of analysts. The analysts were people who, among other things, had to "sort out what was leveraged material." Thonis spoke with conviction about his organization's "conciseness and decisiveness."

Siguler was gone. "Some people," Bing Sung said, "think Putnam shafted Siguler. 'Go to Washington, come back, and run the company. You'll never be a Cabot or Lowell, but . . .'

"Then Putnam left. Clearly, when Siggy left there was an understanding that when he returned he'd have much more power. The implications were all there." Instead, George Putnam had retired and Siguler did not return to the management company, though both were still a presence. Putnam still worked only a block away from the company, and Siguler was frequently called for advice by his former colleagues, many of whom were more relaxed now that they knew they would not have to be accountable to him.

"There's always that enigma about Putnam," Sung continued. "To Siguler, he was almost a father. But Siguler never completely figured him out."

"George Putnam worked for many years for this institution with great enthusiasm," said Derek Bok, who described his relations with Putnam as "cordial." Putnam's successor, Roderick MacDougall, was working full time in an office near Bok's. A 1951 Harvard graduate, MacDougall had just stepped down as chairman of the Bank of New England when the Harvard Corporation selected him.

"I'm not sure how deliberate the process was," MacDougall said. "But the time had come for a change in the role of treasurer." Speaking of himself in the third person, he continued, "The Corporation had several options, including a person who was a professional investment manager. The Corporation chose to go with a broad-based businessman, with exposure to the investment world. The Corporation felt the size and scale of Harvard had grown, debt had increased, the university had taken on some complexities it hadn't in the past."

MacDougall was clearly still fitting into his new role. He spoke about himself and his work carefully. Derek Bok, he said, corrected the grammar in his memos! It was the kind of admission George Putnam would never have made. Little things didn't get to Putnam. If they had, the management company might never have become what it had, and George Siguler would have been sent packing long before.

The banking world MacDougall had left was a "rapidly growing one, where you were always adding assets and people, were forced to make decisions rapidly and so didn't always do the homework you should. The university is unable to cover over its mistakes by doing something new. The need for precision is greater."

Two outside firms were at the time evaluating the risks of trading at the management company, MacDougall reported.

"You can't say," said Walter Cabot, "that constructive planning and administration hurt. I'm sympathetic to what Rod's doing. It's a little of a pain in the ass to me, but we're bigger, more vulnerable to suits, and so on. Remember the power plant? Bok understands that is in the past, but if something like that comes up in the future, he wants to be able to say to Rod, 'When I need you, I need you.' Professional management says something about accountability. Life changes, I think a lot more today about legal stuff. My God, now we've got job descriptions."

One day at the management company, at his corner desk right behind the horseshoe of other trading desks, Bing Sung stared at the screen of his video display terminal. Next to him a trader, a woman, was smoking Newports and drinking a Tab, and another trader, a man, was shooting a Nerf basketball into a miniature basket taped to a large plate-glass window. A phone receiver cradled between his head and one shoulder, Sung shouted, "Break, bonds, break!"

Sung was worried that MacDougall might "cut out the games, which take a lot of management time."

"To be in the forefront of investment opportunities," MacDougall said, "you have to give people a free hand. At the same time, those who oversee have an obligation to understand the risks. Me and others on the Corporation are on a learning curve."

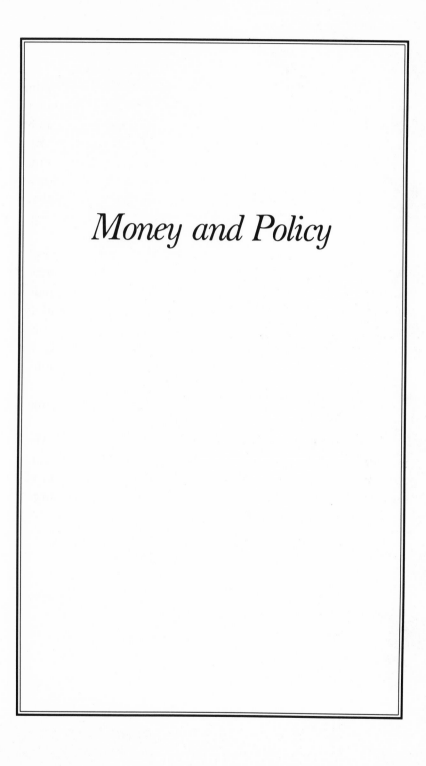

Money and Policy

THE TELEPHONES in Massachusetts Hall began ringing as soon as the report had been released. *The New York Times* called. The major national newsweeklies were planning stories. The report was from the Harvard Corporation's Committee on Shareholder Responsibility (CCSR), composed of Harvard's new treasurer, Roderick MacDougall, and three others, to the Advisory Committee on Shareholder Responsibility (ACSR), a twelve-member group of students, faculty, and alumni. The report, and an accompanying statement by Derek Bok, were released on Valentine's Day of 1985, and it was the second item in the third part of the report that attracted all the attention: "One divestment action: *Baker International Corporation.* In January, on the instruction of the CCSR, the Harvard Management Company sold the University's 60,000 shares in this company."

No issue at Harvard — or on many other American college and university campuses — has so divided opinion since the end of the Vietnam War as the question of South African investments. Harvard's policy on investments in companies that do business in South Africa has evolved over time, but its basic tenets were formulated in 1978, when the Harvard Corporation adopted principles closely akin to those developed in 1977 by the Rev. Leon Sullivan, a Philadelphia minister. Amended in 1984, they state minimum guidelines for the treatment of blacks in the South African workplace. A company doing business in South Africa, if its stock is owned by Harvard, must subscribe to the Sullivan Principles or have shown it is adhering to practices closely approximating them. The policy has been the subject of more written statements by Bok than anything else in his presidency.

The history of the Corporation's South African actions include several significant events, such as the 1981 decision to sell $51 million in Citibank securities because that bank had lent money to the government of South Africa. But during the long debate at Harvard over divestment, the university had never before sold its stock in a company doing business in South Africa because of that company's nonadherence to Harvard's investment policy. There was much else in the Baker report about "dialogues" between Harvard and other companies, and Bok's statement, reviewing Harvard's policy, noted that he served as chairman of the National Council of the South African Education Program, which, Bok said, "brings each year 80–90 non-white South Africans to begin studying in the United States." But it was the Baker divestment that received all the notice, and Roderick MacDougall, for one, was impressed.

"Everything in the report had to be absolutely pure," he said. MacDougall took many of the media calls himself. "They were scary questions," he said.

When in 1984 the CCSR refused to accept an ACSR recommendation of total divestment, the announcement was headlined across the top of the front page of the next day's *Boston Globe,* and a red rectangle was printed around the headline. A 1985 *Boston Globe Magazine* article about divestment was illustrated on the cover with a color photograph of Harvard seniors at commencement wearing mortarboards on which were printed two messages: "Divest," "Divest Now." *The New York Times,* in its issue of February 15, 1985, ran a story on the front page of the business section headlined "South Africa Stock Sale by Harvard," and the story was given a page-one peg.

Before the Baker report was issued, Bok had drafted a long internal memo on the subject. "Were we aware of the power, and the consequences?" MacDougall asked rhetorically, his soft-spoken, almost hushed voice finally becoming animated. "Damn right we were."

Almost a year had passed since the ACSR had, by a six to five vote (with one abstention), recommended total divestiture. To the surprise of no one, the CCSR had not accepted that advice, which gave its subsequent Baker International divestment added prominence.

"Dialogue with this company, begun in June, 1984, had been suspended shortly thereafter when the company left the portfolio," the February 14, 1985, CCSR report on the Baker divestment had stated.

> The dialogue was re-initiated after the stock was purchased once again in December, 1984.
>
> The result of this dialogue was a CCSR conclusion that the company would not, in the foreseeable future, provide Harvard with information and data sufficient to support the company's earlier assertion that Baker International — while refusing to report required data to the Sullivan organization or pay the required fee for an annual monitoring/reporting by the Arthur D. Little Company — was nevertheless "achieving all the goals of the Reverend Sullivan."
>
> In dialogues with companies under Harvard's existing policy on divestment, Harvard has long taken the position that a company refusing to participate in the Sullivan reporting process must undertake a considerable burden of disclosure to interested shareholders if it is to demonstrate that it is adhering to reasonable ethical standards in its South Africa operations.
>
> The relatively small amount of specific data which Baker International was willing to provide Harvard did not persuade the

CCSR that Baker subsidiaries in South Africa were adhering to reasonable standards with respect to efforts to improve the welfare of nonwhite employees, their families and their communities. It should also be noted that Baker management advised the CCSR that the company would be unwilling to undertake any form of explicit opposition to the influx control laws (which constrain where nonwhites may live and work). Harvard urges such opposition by companies in its portfolio.

Like one of the questions raised by Harvard's acceptance of government research money, divestment of stock for political purposes was seen by Bok as an invitation to others to meddle in Harvard's academic life. "In order to protect the process of learning and discovery," he had written,

universities must maintain a reasonable autonomy in the conduct of their internal affairs. They must persuade the outside world to refrain from exerting pressure that would limit the freedom of their members to speak and publish as they choose. They must also preserve the freedom to select the best teachers and scholars for the faculty regardless of their opinions or political activities and to set their own policies without external control save by the government in behalf of established public ends. . . . We cannot expect individuals and organizations to respect our right to speak and write and choose our members as we think best if we insist on using institutional sanctions to try to impose on *them* those policies and opinions that *we* consider important.

Covering every conceivable base in his arguments, anticipating the response of his critics and including in his statements his response to the questions he expected, a typical Bok statement on South Africa was a tour de force of legal reasoning. The prose was even, clear, and dispassionate — always dispassionate.

Every year, shareholder resolutions are introduced to bar corporate support to universities on grounds such as those just mentioned [Harvard's position on ROTC, or the university's policies concerning involvement in covert CIA activities]. These resolutions are regularly defeated because most shareholders are persuaded that corporations should not use economic leverage to influence the internal policies of universities. It would be unreasonable to expect such attitudes to continue if we begin boycotting products or selling shares to press particular policies on corporations and other organizations.

Some of the strongest proponents of divestment are not deterred by this prospect. Indeed, they have organized a fund to be given to Harvard only if it agrees to sell its stock in companies doing business in South Africa. I could not disagree more with this approach. Once we enter a world in which those with money and power feel free to exert leverage to influence university policies, we should not be surprised to find that universities have lost much of their valuable independence.

There was no debate about Bok's personal feelings on apartheid; he was quite clear about that. "All of us on every side of the divestment issue agree that apartheid is a cruel and shameful form of racial exploitation that has no conceivable justification," he wrote. And, on divestment, he stressed that "My views on this matter are not casual; they involve the essential purposes of the university and the terms on which it exists and does its work in our society."

At the heart of Bok's own argument against divestiture was his repeatedly stated belief that it would not accomplish what proponents said it would. The CCSR, too, had said the same, though not in as much detail as Bok. Far more space was allocated in CCSR reports to summaries of Harvard's proxy votes and to the results of its "dialogues" with various companies that, for one reason or another, hadn't met Harvard's South African standards. It was within the format of such a regular report that Harvard revealed it had sold stock in Baker International Corporation.

Had Harvard decided that the sheer paperwork involved in making all these reports, and the time consumed by monitoring various companies and following up with correspondence was a poor investment of university resources, South African divestment would have taken place long before. The CCSR, chaired by Hugh Calkins, employed Harvard's associate vice president of public affairs, Michael Blumenfield '55, as its secretary, and a notebook of the committee's relevant correspondence was made available at the end of each academic year at the reference desk of one of the principal undergraduate libraries, Lamont Library. The full texts of CCSR and ACSR reports, as well as statements by Bok, ran in *The Harvard University Gazette,* and an issue of that paper following a major report often contained several thousand words on the subject.

Early in the 1970s, when divestment was first becoming a serious issue at Harvard, George Siguler asked Jim Meketa, "Suppose Harvard were to divest fully of all its holdings on the IRRC [Investors Responsibility Research Center] list. If Harvard complied fully, what would happen to the endowment over the long run?"

Meketa, who recalls that there were about three hundred companies on the IRRC list, began with the companies that made up Standard and Poor's 500. He weeded out all those that were on the IRRC list, plus several other, smaller companies, and then built a "shadow portfolio" of about 250 to 300 issues with characteristics that closely approximated those in the Harvard endowment — characteristics such as yield, growth, and stability. Then, using computer programs he devised for the assignment, he "back-tested" this hypothetical portfolio, trying to see what Harvard's present endowment would be had Harvard owned such hypothetical listings one, three, or five years before.

"We found it was very difficult to track," he says. "Some stocks were deviating randomly. It was a crude approximation, too, since we couldn't really know what the portfolio managers would have done." He could not make his "shadows" as stable as the real Harvard portfolio was. But he was still able to draw some conclusions.

"We felt divestment posed some dangers. In some periods, the portfolio might have have had a *better* return — for example, in the period of the late sixties and early seventies. Certain small companies were booming then, and there were many such companies in our model. But we felt that trend was peaking, and we were right. Would the portfolio have done worse? It's impossible to answer with any intellectual honesty and rigor."

Imagine that every major institution in the United States divested of all its South African holdings at once. What would be the result?

"It couldn't happen in the real world without government intervention. But — there would be a massive, one-time transfer of wealth. The stocks in those companies would go down, other people would buy them, the prices would go back up. There'd be lots of dollars going to brokers!"

When someone asks of Harvard's investment and other policies, "Who's making decisions?" the answer is the President and Fellows of Harvard College. This ancient body, also known as the Harvard Corporation, chooses its own members, who are then approved by the "Honorable and Reverend" Board of Overseers, Harvard's other governing body. Though Harvard is officially run by both groups, only an overseer believes his board is more than ceremonial. The thirty-member Board of Overseers, elected by alumni, meets six times a year and looks into various academic and administrative matters, including financial policy, through an elaborate committee system. But the overseers never make an important decision by themselves and usually simply rubber stamp whatever the President and Fellows of Harvard College decide.

On May 5, 1985, for example, an overseers' ad hoc Committee on Harvard's Performance in Voting its Stock issued a report supporting the Corporation's policy. "Harvard University," the committee concluded, "as a leading institution of higher education, has an important obligation to exercise shareholder responsibility and to take humane and responsible positions, while at the same time maintaining sound financial practices. These goals are not necessarily in conflict. . . . The recent Progress Report by the CCSR, concerning divestment of one company and improvements linked to University dialogues with other companies, indicates that the University policy on divestment is effective."

The Harvard Alumni Association manages the election of overseers. The association usually doles out the sought-after honor of being nominated to alumni who have been active in Harvard affairs, especially fund raising. Once members are elected, the association has less direct involvement, though one of the standing committees of the board has to do with alumni affairs and development.

The six overseers' meetings each year take up twelve days, and an overseer spends eight days on a visiting committee. Overseers quickly learn how little real power they have. The title, however, has such a lordly ring to it that most members put up and shut up, hoping their service will earn them consideration the next time there's a vacancy on the Corporation. Such hope is usually in vain, for the fellows tend to hold office for long terms and in nearly three and a half centuries of corporate existence have never invited a woman or minority member to join them.

Harvard's overseers, most of them business or professional people, represent the prosperity but not the diversity of Harvard alumni. A prominent group of men and women, the board in 1984–85 consisted of Robert R. Barker, managing partner, Robert R. Barker & Co.; Leo L. Beranek, founder, Bolt, Beranek, and Newman, Inc.; Barry Bingham, chairman of the board, Courier-Journal and Louisville Times Company; Joan T. Bok, chairwoman and director, New England Electric System; Mrs. John M. Bradley, trustee; Lewis M. Branscomb, vice president and chief scientist, IBM Corporation; Samuel C. Butler, partner, Cravath, Swaine & Moore; Theodore Chase, counsel, Palmer & Dodge; Saul G. Cohen, professor of chemistry, Brandeis University; George C. Dillon, chairman of the board and chief executive officer, Butler Manufacturing Company; Donna R. Ecton, vice president, Campbell Soup Company; Peter C. Goldmark Jr., executive director, Port Authority of New York and New Jersey;

Peter S. Heller, partner, Webster & Sheffield; Arnold Hiatt, chairman of the board, chief executive officer, and president, Stride Rite Corporation; George D. Langdon Jr., president, Colgate University; George N. Leighton, judge, U.S. District Court, Chicago; Augustus P. Loring, professional trustee; A. Theodore Lyman Jr., director and trustee, former vice president of the Putnam Management Company, Inc.; Anne M. Morgan, trustee and community volunteer; William A. Oates, rector emeritus, St. Paul's School; Mauricio T. Obregón, chancellor, University of the Andes; Roderic B. Park, vice chancellor, University of California at Berkeley; Richard S. Ross, M.D., dean, the Johns Hopkins University School of Medicine; Peter J. Solomon, managing director and chairman of mergers and acquisitions department, Lehman Brothers; Louisa Clark Spencer, trustee and community volunteer; Stephen Stamus, vice president, Exxon Corporation; Gerald E. Thomas, United States ambassador to Kenya; An Wang, chairman of the board and president, Wang Laboratories, Inc.; Denie S. Weil, consultant, nonprofit institutions; and Barry L. Williams, executive assistant to the president, Bechtel Investments, Inc.

Derek Bok and Roderick MacDougall were members of the Board of Overseers ex officio. Joan T. Bok, no relation to Derek Bok, became the second woman to preside over the board in May 1985.

The house at 17 Quincy Street, which President Lowell had built in 1911, became the office of the governing boards exactly sixty years later. Prior to 1971, the overseers met in University Hall and the Corporation in Massachusetts Hall. Except for the Wednesday meeting the day before commencement, the Corporation always meets on Mondays — approximately every other week through the academic year. The overseers never meet with the Corporation, though members of the two groups dine together on occasion.

The house is built of red brick. The trim is white, and green shutters frame the sides of each window. Over the front door is a portico with an iron railing, and a flagpole points out at an angle over the railing. Air conditioners protrude from many of the windows. Pine trees in back define the grounds, but the garden the Puseys had is gone. The space was taken when the adjacent Pusey Library was constructed for Harvard's archives and part of the overflow from Widener.

In one of the second-floor former bedrooms at the top of the staircase, a fireplace, chandelier, leather-bound books, standing clock, and brass lamps contribute to an air of old-worldliness in the office of Robert Shenton, secretary to the Corporation and secretary of the overseers. Only Harvard would place such meaningless stress on two prepositions. Shenton, who sports a moustache, came to his work via experience as Harvard's registrar. About a dozen people work under this shy, orderly man who calls himself a civil servant. On a day when there is no meeting taking place, you can hear Shenton's manual typewriter as you come up the stairs.

If anyone were to question his routine, Shenton said he would "tell them it's been done this way since 1650." The Corporation calendar is scheduled a year in advance, in the spring of the preceding year. Shenton works out the agenda with Bok, Harvard's five vice presidents, and the treasurer and other fellows. Shenton sets up appointments for people meeting with the Corporation and tells them when they should get in their agenda material, which is always mailed to the fellows five days before a Monday meeting. Even a small matter, such as the appointment of a new faculty member, cannot be announced by the news office until the Corporation has made the formal appointment, often many months after the professor has started teaching.

Shenton described the process of Corporation meetings as "a big operation. There is an enormous amount of business." The former master bedroom in which the Corporation meets at 17 Quincy Street has a large table in the center and high-backed leather chairs around it. When the Corporation convenes, the president sits at the head of the table, the treasurer to his right, the senior fellow to his left, and so on. Shenton sits off to a side at a separate table, where he takes the minutes. He never uses a tape recorder to do so, of course. The president, not the senior fellow, presides at meetings.

"I remember being surprised to learn the fellows aren't paid," said Walter Cabot. "That's a vestige of old community service."

"The two-board structure is unusual," President Bok acknowledged, "and I doubt whether many new institutions would choose to adopt it. Like most administrative structures, it can be made to work, given a desire by the people involved to succeed." Bok, who said that "on academic matters, of course, the Corporation tends to defer to the president," partially agreed with the statement of a recent overseers' committee that "the President and Fellows of Harvard College is more nearly a multiple executive." Bok stressed that this was more closely the case "on financial, government, or administrative matters. As universities become more complicated to administer, an increasingly important problem is how to retain the practice of choosing presidents from the ranks of professors and educators and still gain the necessary financial and administrative skills to preside over an extraordinarily complicated and expensive organization. The Harvard Corporation affords an interesting model for addressing this problem."

In 1954, when Nathan Pusey had his first opportunity to nominate someone to the Corporation, he chose Hooks Burr. Pusey remembers saying to him, "You can just attend meetings and sit for five years. But there will come a time when you will be called on for more." Thirty years later, Pusey shook his head in amusement at these words, as he recalled what happened in 1969.

Student protests "arrived at Harvard late, coming east to west from Berkeley," said Burr. "We were damned if we were going to let the institution crumble because of a few loud individuals. Basically what you're trying to do is keep the institution on an even keel. The sum of the institution," he continued, "is its people."

Burr stepped down from the Harvard Corporation in 1982.

"There had been a tradition of fairly long service," he said matter-of-factly.

The State Street Bank building where Burr has his twenty-third-floor office as a senior partner in Ropes & Gray affords him a magnificent view of Boston Harbor and Logan Airport. Burr is an exceedingly soft-spoken, polite man who uses mild profanity. He wears suspenders. Past his usually open door, purposeful-looking men and women walk by on the parquet floors. It is very quiet. His desk is covered with green slips with telephone messages.

Burr used to be a securities lawyer. Then he went to "general business." Now he does a lot of estate work as a trustee. "These things change as a lawyer's friends and he grow older," he said.

Chairman of the Massachusetts General Hospital board, Burr has always given much of his time to what he calls charity work. "There's no doubt that some people do it because it gives them stature. That is a degrading reason to be involved. If that's the case, I think it shows, that you don't have a real commitment." He referred to certain books about the law that advocate this as a way of getting ahead. "Such people don't stick the course," he said. You must "get deeply involved. And the more deeply involved you get, the more difficult it is to get out."

Harvard's governance, Burr said, is "not that difficult, just different. I used to tell people the Corporation was like the executive committee of a board of directors. But that's not quite it either."

In the lovely setting of 17 Quincy Street, so far from the world outside Harvard, the final decision to go ahead with MATEP was made by the Harvard Corporation. Burr, who was the senior fellow then, later blamed the costs on the regulatory process. The protest against MATEP annoyed Burr, though "it's necessary to protect people's rights," he added, with little enthusiasm. His comment was part of a pattern in which no one on the Corporation accepted individual blame for what happened.

*

Number 474 Brookline Avenue is a modern brick and concrete building with large plate-glass windows around much of its perimeter. Next door is the Dana Farber Cancer Institute, and from the sidewalk the two buildings look like they are both part of the same complex of medical schools and teaching hospitals that dominates the landscape of this area of Boston. They are. From far away, what stands out is the new building's 312-foot-tall concrete smokestack; from just across the street, you notice the four concrete cooling towers sticking up above the roof; with your face pressed against the windows, the most startling sight is that of six giant diesel engines. On a sign by the main door, which a security officer and four closed-circuit television monitors guard, the building is identified as the Cogeneration Management Company. This is the corporate name of MATEP, the acronym for Medical Area Total Energy Plant.

From a purely technological standpoint, what is inside this building and what it is supposed to do is impressive. Constructed to replace a 1907 powerhouse on Blackfan Street, two blocks from the new building, MATEP, Harvard's official literature states, "is designed to provide reliable, energy-efficient, and environmentally safe sources of steam, chilled water, and electricity for six Harvard affiliated teaching hospitals and medical research centers as well as for the University's Medical School, School of Public Health, and School of Dental Medicine. The plant also provides steam for Mission Park, a 775-unit mixed-income housing development, and the Massachusetts College of Art." To do this, MATEP has three steam boilers, two heat recovery steam generators, five chillers, two steam turbines, and the six diesel engines, plus many state of the art antipollution devices. At full operation, MATEP could produce sixty-four megawatts of electricity, 900,000 pounds per hour of steam, and nearly twenty thousand tons per hour of chilled water. A key to the plant's efficiency is its use of cogeneration, in which electricity and steam are produced simultaneously.

MATEP's history is a long series of construction delays and

cost overruns, bitter regulatory battles, complex financing plans, behind-the-scenes administrative maneuvers, and endless debate over whether Harvard ever should have gotten into this project in the first place. Few officials at Harvard will claim any credit for MATEP; the subject is usually skirted around. And development officers have had to contend with nagging questions about the Harvard Campaign's being a MATEP bailout, questions that people have raised, in part, because the rising total cost of MATEP so closely paralleled the campaign's fund-raising goal, which was itself revised at about the same time Harvard issued a major MATEP bond issue.

The people most personally affected by the actual construction of the plant are the residents of the area and nearby Brookline, where several Harvard alumni were prominent in the protest. Their feelings against MATEP are strong. John Grady, a professor of sociology at Wheaton College and resident of Mission Hill, said with resignation, "We've lost the fight." But his voice rose as he recalled the neighborhood's initial reaction to the plans in 1975, and he questioned with precise figures how Harvard could have calculated then that MATEP would save money. "Unless they get a government bailout, they blew two hundred and fifty million dollars!" says Professor Grady. "Who's making any decisions anywhere?"

In a lengthy article on MATEP published in the July–August 1980 issue of *Harvard Magazine,* editor John Bethell traces MATEP to the 1972 formation of a group called the Medical Area Service Corporation, "which would validate the need for a central power plant, and take part in its planning and development." Shortly thereafter, a New York engineering firm, working on a consulting basis for Harvard, estimated the construction cost of such a plant at $50 million. Harvard acquired more property in the area around the plant's proposed construction, and there were several steps in getting the proper zoning. State and city agencies were involved in the early regulatory decisions, and Harvard changed engineers. Construction began in November

1976, just as the financial vice president at the time, Hale Champion, was chosen by newly elected president Jimmy Carter as undersecretary of health, education, and welfare.

"If there's a guy who's responsible," the cigar-smoking Champion said long afterward, "I'm the one. Boston Edison stonewalled us." Harvard, he maintained, had tried to work with the electric company and had been forced into going on the project alone. This, he recalled, made the Harvard Corporation "uncomfortable."

Community opposition, which had been generating steam of its own, surfaced on several fronts at once. Harvard was able to strike a deal with one group, promising to construct the Mission Park housing project, with free heat from MATEP, in return for support of MATEP. This agreement, made in such a lordly manner, appeased some local residents and outraged others. Then, in Brookline, Bethell reports, a committee "produced a report that gave MATEP an unclean bill of health." In January of 1977, Harvard applied to the state's Department of Environmental Quality Engineering (DEQE) for the necessary air-quality approval, following which the legal proceedings of hearings, rulings, and court cases became labyrinthian, still unresolved at the time Bethell's piece appeared — though by then the steam and chilled-water portion of the plant had been constructed.

Four years later, the focus of debate over MATEP had come down to one issue: the potential health hazard of the nitrogen dioxide emitted by the diesel engines. In September 1984, a state-appointed hearing officer issued a report that stated, "The risk attributable to MATEP could effect an increase of between 0.01 percent and 0.1 percent to the annual risk of contracting lung cancer of a 40-year-old male continuously exposed for 20 years to MATEP emissions. The above level is equivalent to smoking between one puff and one cigarette (or 1.4 cigarettes) per year for 20 years." The use of the decimal point in the cigarette figure, one Harvard official said, was a "classic example of making a silly speculation appear precise and scientific." The report was affirmed by DEQE the following January, which meant Harvard could now begin *testing* the diesel engines.

"We are, of course, pleased that the state environmental agency has once again supported our long-held belief that MATEP is safe," Harvard's vice president for administration, Robert H. Scott, said in a prepared statement. "The safety of the plant now has been confirmed by each of a long series of decisions that DEQE made concerning MATEP." Others were not so pleased, and further judicial review was forthcoming. Moreover, with the slowing of inflation and the stabilization of fuel costs, MATEP for the moment no longer appeared to be a good economic bet, even had the diesel-engine portion of the plant not been idled during the regulatory reviews, and even with the creative use of tax-exempt financing Harvard devised to fund the costs. Assuming the diesel engines passed muster, and discounting the impact of further regulatory delay, MATEP was still, Scott admitted, "going to look expensive for a long time."

Shortly before *Harvard Magazine* was going to press with its story about MATEP, editor John Bethell received a telephone call from Andrew Heiskell. The Corporation had just learned of the pending article, and Heiskell, Bethell recalls, "asked politely if it wasn't a good idea for a lawyer to look at the piece."

"Oh, shit," Bethell thought, fearing he was in for a fight.

Long before Andrew Heiskell called him that day in early June 1980, Bethell had firmly established a reputation for his magazine as a kind of *Smithsonian Magazine* with a Harvard accent. Bethell prided himself on its editorial independence. Andrew Heiskell was as imposing an opponent as Bethell could have encountered. On the thirty-fifth floor of the Time-Life building in Manhattan, Heiskell has an office suite he has shared with his secretary since his 1982 retirement as chairman of Time Inc. A tall man, elegantly dressed, with a full head of well-groomed hair, Heiskell is a presence, a man who dominates a conversation or meeting.

Before he became a fellow, Heiskell was president of the overseers. At the age of sixty-nine, Heiskell was expected to announce his resignation from the Corporation upon reaching his next birthday. With Hugh Calkins already stepping down, Charles P. Slichter, Harvard '45 and a solid-state physicist at the University of Illinois Center for Advanced Study, would become the senior fellow. Coleman M. Mockler Jr., Harvard '52 and the chairman and chief executive officer of the Gillette Company, was the youngest member of the Corporation, with the exception of Derek Bok. No biographical information about fellows is provided by the Corporation. "We don't keep biographies of fellows on file," a secretary at 17 Quincy Street said. "Look them up in *Who's Who.*"

Heiskell began his career as a reporter for *The New York Tribune,* where he also worked on the city desk. Science editor of *Life* magazine at the age of twenty-two, he quickly rose through the corporate ranks. He claims credit for starting *People,* which he thought "might be reasonably successful." He still works a fifty-hour week; among his other voluntary posts is chairman of the New York Public Library board of trustees. He was planning a trip to Egypt with his wife, Marian Sulzberger Heiskell, whose family owns *The New York Times.* "I'll slow down when the system slows me down," Heiskell said of his activities. "I have ideas. It's difficult not to be able to do [all of] them." For Thanksgiving, he was taking twenty-three children and grandchildren to a resort.

Hands behind his head, jacket off, the cufflinks on his striped shirt shining, Heiskell put his feet up on the desk. There was a television in his office, and by a long couch a coffee table with copies of *People* and *Time.* Some of the artwork on the walls was modern, and a photograph of Heiskell and President Kennedy hung with several paintings. There is a view of the Hudson from Heiskell's office, and he sometimes stared out at it through his horn-rimmed glasses.

Running for overseer in 1973 "was a sheer fluke," said Heiskell, who'd spent one year in the 1930s at Harvard Business

School and "hated it." He left the Business School because he "didn't like business. I'm not a country club businessman or a golfing businessman." What kind of businessman was he? "A pretty good one. But it doesn't take up every minute of my life. I don't go around discussing profit and loss."

Now, from his position as a member of the Corporation, which he described as a "marvel — it's so anonymous — the only voice is that of the president" — he had adopted its paternalistic posture toward Harvard. He thought of the Corporation as "closer to a cabinet for the president, rather than as a board."

The Harvard Corporation, he continued, was "the equivalent of the Governor's Council in precabinet days." It was composed of "people with whom the president can speak freely. There won't be leaks. There aren't the repercussions there are bound to be on a bigger board." The Corporation, he explained, dealt with "management problems," whereas it was "issues" that come before the overseers.

"When a problem is resolved by the Corporation," he said, "it goes to the overseers for their approval." There were ten to fifteen items on a typical agenda for a Corporation meeting. At most, one is an issue to be referred to the overseers.

Harvard post-Pusey had created "far better administration. You have to have people who can deal with legislatures, the community . . . and, what the hell, we are a big business, we have to act like one," he added, apparently forgetting MATEP.

"One of the advantages of the Corporation's being very small and reasonably stable is that you don't get into adversarial relationships. We talk with the president. He takes our advice or doesn't. At least he knows he's getting the best advice these particular people can give."

Before the Corporation's misgivings about the MATEP article in *Harvard Magazine* came up, the magazine's own lawyer, John Taylor Williams, had already looked at the piece, which tried to present a factual account of how Harvard had gotten into this problem and how it might get out.

Bethell had lunch with Heiskell the day after he was called. "We were at loggerheads," Bethell says. Bethell talked with Vice President Daniel Steiner, his Harvard classmate and a director of the magazine.

"Dan was pretty satisfied with the story. But he thought it was a good idea if we could assure the Corporation. He read the piece, and in the end so did all the directors. . . . It worked out fine, with only a number and one quotation changed, the latter because the person to whom it was attributed said it had been truncated, which was true." Bethell never again heard from Heiskell. He looks back at the episode as "a case study that is of credit to Harvard."

A reader of the story might come to a different conclusion. "How does it feel to have a 73-megawatt headache?" the piece's headline asked. "The members of the Harvard Corporation know," a subhead stated. In the meticulously researched text that followed, Bethell couched what he said in terms that were sympathetic to the Corporation. "Because the Fellows of Harvard College have outside responsibilities," he wrote, "their concern with MATEP has limits." Later, he wrote that they "might regret the day they got into the business of generating power." The whole episode was a case of "unanticipated results." Perhaps the protest was unanticipated. But the university's response to it was predictable.

Harvard had closed ranks on what could have been a public relations disaster. More than money was at stake here; Harvard's reputation was on the line. "Harvard's governors thought hard before going ahead," Bethell wrote. What he did not say was that much of that thinking took place at a climactic meeting at Ropes & Gray, after which George Siguler, among others, almost resigned because of his opposition to the MATEP plans. Nor did Bethell or any other Harvard official publicly discuss the surplus cash MATEP used and the effect that had on the management company, which had to be a little more conservative than it might have. The "flap" over Bethell's article wasn't a flap at all. The real flap was the MATEP decision, but Harvard's name came to the rescue, protecting the men who made the decision.

"You only enter into situations where you know what the hell you're doing and when to get out," George Siguler believed. Another maxim was, "An organization can't stay static." With its construction of MATEP, Harvard could certainly not be accused of standing still. But Siguler, like many others within and without Harvard, wondered what Harvard was doing in the energy business. Later, working with Tom O'Brien, Harvard's financial vice president, he confronted the financial fallout from MATEP. As the cost of MATEP mounted, and initial plans for leveraged leasing of the project fell through, Harvard was stuck with a lemon larger than the plant itself: the bill.

Harvard, to use Siguler's phrase, has "unusual name credibility." That was one reason the management company had been able to attract investment professionals who might otherwise have been unwilling to work for a university. It was also why Harvard had had its way with MATEP. Now, with MATEP a reality, Harvard had to use its good name for a related purpose: debt financing.

Bond rates vary for a variety of reasons, but, in general, the longer the term of the bond, the higher the rate of interest, since the value of the dollar far in the future is difficult to predict. A rise in present interest rates depresses the bond market, since the investment is less attractive; correspondingly, a decrease in rates makes bonds a more sought-after investment. In 1982, when Harvard wanted to sell tax-exempt bonds for MATEP through the Massachusetts Health and Educational Facilities Authority, interest rates were very high. With O'Brien's support, Siguler hit on a solution. He called it a one-three-five put bond.

"I had a close relationship with George Siguler," said O'Brien afterward. "We became close friends. We would bounce around the financial affairs of the university. We worked very closely on strategic issues of finance at the university.

"The one-three-five put structure at the time was very creative. Siguler was very smart. A lot of smart people are not proactive. But Siguler said, 'Let's do it.' "

Siguler's recollection of the one-three-five put bonds is specific and cloaked in the jargon of his profession. "You write the stated maturity of the bond in a contract," he says. "Say thirty years, payable semiannually. There is a yield curve; segmented out, those last years are quite expensive. We wanted the protection of very long money, but participation at the short end where rates are cheaper. A thirty-year piece of paper with a buy back — a one-year put bond — that's what we did."

Harvard, Siguler was saying, wanted as low an interest rate as possible, but it wanted to do this while still getting long-term financing. But, given the bond market at the time, no rational investor was going to give Harvard such a deal without some protection for himself. The put option gave the investor such security; if interest rates continued to climb, he could "put" the bonds back to Harvard, which would then have had to refinance at the new, higher rate. This was the risk Harvard took; in return for doing so, the rate of the first bond issue was three percentage points lower than it would have been otherwise, which saved Harvard about $7 million a year.

The bonds earned the "one-three-five" terminology because they were "putable" on the first, third, and fifth anniversaries of their issue (and each subsequent anniversary afterward). Harvard expected interest rates would come down, and it planned to refinance the bonds then — which is exactly what happened.

"Clearly," Siguler continued, "the concern is that a school is going to borrow beyond the means to finance the debt. Yes, Harvard's debt is large, but it could go in tomorrow and write a check for the entire amount.

"Compare Harvard to a regulated bank, where the ratio of debt to assets is roughly twenty to one. By those standards, Harvard could take on debt to make itself a fifty-billion-dollar institution! And that's just with respect to endowment. Think of the rare books in Houghton Library, the paintings at the Fogg Art Museum, the physical plant, and the 'futures unlisted' — the people still to give." Siguler's calculation, taking Harvard's endowment and multiplying it by twenty to arrive at the total, was hypothetical and meant to amuse.

"I manage liabilities," Tom O'Brien said, "and the management company manages assets." A few days before, Harvard had refinanced a large portion of the original one-three-five put bonds, which were issued in 1982. The original issue, known as Series E, had been to raise funds for a variety of projects, including the House renovations that were a goal of the Harvard Campaign. Series G, which followed, were the MATEP bonds: $350 million to refinance construction and interest costs. By early 1985, Harvard's total bond debt was in excess of $600 million more than that of any other such institution in the country.

The refinancing option, which had been planned all along, was simply a case of "long-term, tax-exempt money versus short," O'Brien continued. "Could we afford the risk of borrowing short, until the rates came down?" The answer was a clear yes, and O'Brien could say now, "It was a prudent calculation to wait until the yield curve became flatter.

"Why have borrowed in the first place? The House system needed renovation," O'Brien began, adding, "You don't let the buildings fall down. And the room rates will carry the debt." In other words, part of a student's term bill for room reflected the cost of the money borrowed for the renovations. "Was there any risk that Harvard can't fill all the rooms?" O'Brien asked as though it were a rhetorical question. He answered anyway with a firm, "No. A risk that the cost of education will get too high? Okay, but if Harvard let the buildings fall down, are we going to do the best science in the world? Can we afford not to?"

O'Brien was feeling relieved. He compared the situation to that of a homeowner who'd taken out a mortgage at a time when the rates were higher than he liked. Finally, the rates come down to a level the homeowner thinks is reasonable. When that happens, he refinances.

The subject of the bonds inevitably led back to MATEP. O'Brien sighed. "Some engineers say when we look back on it, we'll look very good," O'Brien said. "Some financial people say, 'You took a hell of a hit.'" Others believed that Harvard had made lemonade from a very expensive lemon.

The money Harvard saved with its one-three-five put bonds freed it from having to take the funds from elsewhere, through an additional tuition increase or from endowment earnings. Moreover, it enabled Harvard to retain ownership of its real property; nothing had to be pledged as security. The money Harvard saved from issuing tax-exempt bonds in the first place, instead of resorting to some other means of financing, came from the United States taxpayer. Usually, investors in a high tax bracket buy tax-exempt bonds, and the taxes they would have paid on a different kind of investment represent a loss to the government that is made up elsewhere.

Harvard was never able to convince all its alumni that the Harvard Campaign was somehow not entwined with MATEP. Sophisticated donors asked about it, and no matter how Harvard explained it, no matter how clearly it showed that its debt service was being carried as part of a balanced budget, the fact remained that, without MATEP, Harvard's present financial condition would be even better.

George Putnam, who had angered Bok when he told a *Boston Globe* reporter that he'd always been opposed to MATEP, never accepted responsibility for it. Harvard's independent treasurer, like the other fellows, was not publicly accountable. Instead, in private, Putnam was able to lean on his old friend, Governor Edward King, with the hope that the regulators assigned to study MATEP were not hostile to Harvard. And Putnam backed Siguler in his one-three-five put bond proposal. Managing the debt would be Tom O'Brien's problem — and Rod MacDougall's.

Working at first out of a small, temporary office on the second floor of 17 Quincy Street, MacDougall had been uncertain whether he would eventually make his main office in Boston. For one thing, in an expansion of the treasurer's administrative duties, he would be devoting more of his time to the job than had Putnam, who never, during his tenure, had given up his work for the Putnam Management Company. The shift in scope that this enlargement represented was the result of a decision by the Corporation to pave the way for the selection of an academic as Derek Bok's successor, whenever that time might come. Smoking Marlboro Lights as he read old treasurer's reports in his tiny room, MacDougall gave no indication that he was aware of such thinking.

A 1951 graduate of Harvard College, MacDougall worked for the Morgan Guaranty Trust Company in New York and the Marine Midland Bank in Rochester, New York, before becoming president of New England Merchants Bank in 1974. The bank, which later changed its name to Bank of New England, appointed him chief executive officer in 1976 and chairman in 1978. MacDougall was also a board member of several other businesses, and he was active in civic affairs, serving the Boston Symphony Orchestra as treasurer and the Massachusetts United Way as chairman, among other volunteer posts. It had taken the Harvard Corporation two years to find him.

Eight months after stepping down as chairman of Bank of New England and succeeding George Putnam as Harvard's twenty-eighth treasurer, MacDougall had a desk in Boston at the Harvard Management Company, but there was now no question where his headquarters were. He had moved into Massachusetts Hall.

Brushing a cigarette ash off his suit, MacDougall paused, as if to enjoy in anticipation the irony of his first remark. His office was lit only by the sunlight of this late February morning. "Things have come up," he said, "that have kept me busy. South Africa, donors with questions about the endowment, assistance to Walter Cabot, working with the management company and development office on unusual gifts, such as those involving com-

plex stock options, chairing the debt management committee";
MacDougall recited a long list. A white handkerchief stuck out
above the top of his suitcoat's outer breast pocket. Harvard was
getting his services, he added, "at a small cost."

Described by someone who knew him as "much more relaxed
than he was at the bank," MacDougall seemed surprised to learn
that George Siguler had been involved in such activities as de-
vising the one-three-five put bonds. He raised his eyebrows over
it.

MacDougall and George Putnam weren't close friends, but
they had had, MacDougall said, "two lengthy meetings." ·
MacDougall telephoned Putnam on occasion.

"There is confusion about Harvard's organization. Harvard
has somehow learned to survive without organization charts.
The key is people who want to work together.

"Clearly the basic skills to run an organization are here. Derek
is a broad-based manager. He's not a typical college or university
president. So there's no need for me to reinforce that."

MacDougall had already cut out several of his outside activities, retaining only his corporate directorships and a few community obligations. He was theoretically devoting two-thirds of
his time to being treasurer of Harvard, but it was far more than
that, he said, "if you defined time as a nine-to-five day."

Choosing his words carefully, MacDougall clasped the side
rungs of the Harvard captain's chair in which he sat. "You can't
jeopardize the family jewels," he said. Looking at the clock, he
said he was going to be late for a directors' meeting in Boston.

MacDougall had already reached the outside door of Massachusetts Hall before abruptly turning around. "Got to get something to read on the subway," he said.

By April 4, the day of Jesse Jackson's second 1985 visit to
Harvard, MacDougall had a clear, sure grasp of the stakes he
was playing for. Historically, the title of treasurer had always
been a misnomer; once appointed by the governor of Massachusetts, the treasurer was now, like the president, selected by the

Corporation and approved by the overseers. But he did not report to a financial vice president, and his power was second only to that of the president. It was a difficult power to define because of the nature of the institution; MacDougall's constituency was much broader than it had been at the bank, and the decisions he made were judged by a much different audience.

MacDougall could now speak fluently about the kind of problems he was dealing with and, if they all were related to money and Harvard, they were nevertheless not parochial. Questions about the management of Harvard's endowment, about the management company's performance and its future, and the relationship of endowment management to fund raising and to the management of Harvard's other assets and its large debt were critical not just to Harvard but, in the view of MacDougall and many others, to the future of private higher education in the country.

Once a year, a committee meets to set the university's spending rate. The committee includes MacDougall, Tom O'Brien, Bok, and three outside people. "O'Brien does the homework on this." Harvard professor Martin Feldstein, former chairman of the President's Council of Economic Advisors, is on the committee. The management company allocates its resources to meet the requirements.

MacDougall's endowment concerns focused on asset allocation. He talked about the "constraints of ownership" and whether "scale" is a problem.

About the university's debt, MacDougall stressed, "There is MATEP, and there is everything else. Clearly, history will credit Derek Bok with making significant investments in the physical plant. Huge dollars went into the Houses. That was unglamorous, and some of it was catch-up, which is a tougher thing to undertake.

"It would clearly have been irresponsible for Harvard not to have taken advantage of tax-exempt financing. It would have been an unfair burden on students and potential donors. Having made the decision, do you do the financing conventionally, or go short-term, because the long-term rates are so high at the time? The put bonds were a little twist; the important decision was to go short-term rather than long." The focus on strategy apparently obviated criticism of Harvard's excessive use of tax-exempt bonds to pay for MATEP.

"MATEP was separate. Again, it would have been irresponsible not to have used financing. The amount of interest-rate coverage is supported by Harvard's income. The coverage ratio is not out of line, and the marketplace says so. Harvard has maintained its triple-A rating.

"The debt service is built into the long-range plans of all the 'tubs.' Repayment is built in. Harvard has not concluded that it's at its debt capacity. Based on what we're told, there is additional capacity. The exact numbers are extremely difficult to quantify, and will grow as the debt is repaid and income increases."

Jim Meketa called Harvard's debt financing "leveraging the Harvard name. You've got to have not just the assets, but the people," he said. "Harvard has a great network." By using its name and network and successfully exploiting the instrument of tax-exempt financing, which was not created by Congress as a bailout for an institution that may have made a financial mistake, Harvard had avoided what could have been a financial disaster. And Harvard's governors, who were not accountable within the institution, had been saved again from shouldering the responsibility of their decisions.

Pale pink, light green, yellow, and white balloons blew in the breeze of a warm mid-February afternoon. The balloons were tied to lampposts, traffic meters, and the grates of the iron fence along the Massachusetts Avenue perimeter of Harvard Yard. In black capital letters, printed on each balloon, was the name of the singing star and actor, Cher, who was in Cambridge to receive the Hasty Pudding Club's award as 1985 Woman of the Year. Preceding the clubhouse ceremonies, which included the presentation of three scenes from the 137th annual Hasty Pudding Theatricals show, *Witch and Famous,* Cher rode in a Lincoln Continental convertible in a procession past a large crowd of cheering onlookers. Dressed in an outfit that included a mink-tail hat, she waved and smiled and posed for countless photographs, and when the parade was over she termed it "a blast."

No such word enlivened the vocabulary of Derek Bok, who, with his new vice president for government, community, and public affairs, John Shattuck, had the day before lunched with Senator Daniel Patrick Moynihan in Washington, D.C. Moynihan had been a Harvard professor before his election to the Senate, and Bok, serving a year's term as chairman of the Association of American Universities, was in Washington for a meeting of that group's executive committee. Shattuck, a Yale-trained lawyer who for eight years was director of the American Civil Liberties Union's Washington office, had set up the luncheon date with Senator Moynihan. Since his Harvard appointment the year before, which had become effective July 1, Shattuck had been splitting his time between Washington and Cambridge. While still with the ACLU, he had started coming up to Cambridge a day or two a week to begin his Harvard work, and now, having completed the transition, he flew to Washington once a week on behalf of Harvard.

Bright, personable, and articulate, Shattuck had plunged into his new duties with enthusiasm and confidence. In a speech before the twenty-five-hundred-member Harvard Club of Washington, he had joked about his appointment. "Some say I'm a mole from New Haven. Others just say Harvard is getting sloppy!" Then he had succinctly outlined the federal governmental issues facing Harvard, while paying homage to his new boss, whom he called "the outstanding university president in America today." It was the only bit of sycophancy in the speech, which closed with an invitation to those present to "work together in Washington to protect the interests of Harvard and the principles we are discussing here today." Those principles included academic freedom, affirmative action, and federal funding of education through research grants and, indirectly, through tax policies that preserved charitable deductions for gifts.

An extraordinary concern with process now characterized the way administrative decisions were made at Harvard. By 1985, Derek Bok had chaired several hundred ad hoc committees. John Shattuck spoke of the tremendous investment of time that was involved in "the need to consult people on subjects," which Shattuck said could be "overwhelming." Harvard decision making was also made more complex by the existence of the various professional and graduate schools, each with its own deans who control their own budgets.

Stating the case for $20 million for programs for public policy, the Harvard Campaign prospectus argued:

> Despite the complexity of the issues our leaders face, despite the difficulty of managing our public institutions, we have had no tradition of serious, careful preparation for positions of public leadership comparable to the preparation provided for those entering our great private professions. This is the principal missing link in American higher education today. Harvard has undertaken a commitment to supply this vital link.
>
> Although the public sector embraces a wide variety of careers, certain basic skills and problem-solving methods have come to play a significant role in the work of officials holding important policy-making positions throughout government. Harvard has developed a basic curriculum which emphasizes the following: methods of policy analysis drawn from economics, statistics, and computer sciences; principles of management adapted from the Business School to the special environment of the public sector; and a sensitivity to basic values derived from ethics, history, and the best of our legal and constitutional traditions.

Discounting the fact that the campaign case was a fund-raising brochure, not an official policy statement, these words were still a revelation of a way of looking at and dealing with the world. They describe something more than a brief for the Kennedy School of Government, the primary — but not the only — beneficiary of this campaign component.

By early December of 1984, when proposals by the U.S. Treasury Department and others for tax reform had been promulgated, Harvard was ready to wage war in Washington. By itself, in concert with other universities and organizations that depended in part on charitable gifts — what many, including Harvard, called the charitable community — and through various institutional associations, Harvard knew exactly where it stood with respect to such proposals and it was prepared to fight them.

John Shattuck had a lengthy memorandum for every important subject that came up in a conversation about his work.

- December 3, 1984, "Impact of the Treasury Tax Reform Proposal on Charitable Giving to Universities," sixteen pages.
- December 11, 1984, "A Comparison of the Costs and Potential Economic Benefits of the Treasury Proposal on Charitable Giving," twenty-eight pages, including three-page "executive summary."
- December 1984, "Key Tax Issues Affecting Higher Education," forty-seven pages, plus ten-page table, "Tax Reform Bills Introduced in the 98th Congress."
- January 1985, "Federal Restrictions on the Free Flow of Academic Information and Ideas," thirty-two pages.
- Undated, "Federal Student Aid Loan Program Dollars Received by Harvard/Radcliffe Students," four pages.
- Undated, "A Proactive Approach Toward Community Affairs," eight pages.

The detail in these memos was encyclopedic:

Tax-exempt bond financing becomes particularly important in an era of high interest rates because they allow an institution to build at lower interest rates when a project is needed rather than when adequate funds can be raised. They provide the only kind of transaction available to 501(c)(3) organizations to reduce their construction costs and to retain title to the property. . . .

It seems likely that it will be some time before the impact of the new appraisal requirements on donor generosity is clear and whether the new requirements are effective in ending valuation abuse. However, several development officers are particularly concerned about the impact of appraisal requirements on gifts of closely held stock valued at over $10,000. . . .

The proposed 2 percent floor will make all taxpayers with charitable contributions of less than 2 percent of AGI effectively non-itemizers from the view of the charitable deduction. Simulations performed using 1979 data suggest that roughly 60 percent of all itemizers had charitable deductions below the floor. Thus, 60 percent of all current itemizers would receive no incentive for charitable contributions under the Treasury proposal. A significant number of itemizers in all income classes would be adversely affected with particular effect on taxpayers earning between $20,000 and $50,000. . . .

The paper flow didn't stop there. Shattuck had started a newsletter, *Government Affairs Report,* and the first issue, dated January 10, 1985, included a message from Shattuck ("Since beginning my work as Vice President . . . I have come to believe that the effectiveness of my office would be enhanced by the creation within the University of an informed 'community of interest' on government issues") and articles on tax reform, academic freedom, and student financial aid. Shattuck had accepted a position on the board of the Phillips Brooks House Association, Harvard's community service organization for students, and copies of an eight-page supplement to *The Harvard University Gazette,* written by Deane Lord and focused, in part, on PBH, were available. So, too, were copies of a biweekly compilation of newspaper and magazine articles about Harvard and higher education. Called the "News Sampler," and put together by the news office in Holyoke Center, one recent such sampler, with Shattuck's name and that of his office on the cover, was twenty-six pages in length.

Shattuck himself exuded a sense of importance about what he was doing, and he didn't need to refer to a memo or an article to explain what might happen if Guaranteed Student Loans were eliminated for students from families with incomes of more than $32,500, or how much money Harvard researchers would lose under Reagan proposals to cut National Institute of Health support (which at the time totaled $33.5 million to 247 researchers at the Medical School, the School of Public Health, and the Faculty of Arts and Sciences). It was all in Shattuck's head, as was an extraordinarily comprehensive plan to further Harvard's cause in Cambridge, at the State House in Boston, and in Washington.

"We're a service agency," Shattuck said. "We don't manage. It's important, for example, that all media contacts go through this office." By that, he said, he did not mean that no one spoke to the press without checking first with him. "You can't manage the news, nor should you. The best medicine is sunshine." There was so much going on at Harvard, Shattuck said, that he sometimes felt like a traffic cop.

He lamented society's "search for heroes," which he called "disturbing. There are few to be found, and they don't really have the answers." Derek Bok, he believed, "was very careful to make sure that when he uses the platform [of his presidency], it is effective." For example, in response to a criticism of affirmative action programs written by Charles Murray and published in *The New Republic,* Bok wrote a strong rebuttal in the same magazine a month later. "Universities should stick by their conviction that a judicious concern for race in admitting students," Bok said, "will eventually help to lift the arbitrary burdens that have hampered blacks in striving to achieve their goals in our society."

Bok, Shattuck continued, had made an "enormous contribution in attracting people [to Harvard]." And he had created a "sound, deliberative process for discussion. One of the greatest contributions a Harvard president can make is not to intrude." He should, however, "promote, without becoming a person who is a kind of hero."

Three full-time people under Shattuck worked on federal relations alone, and one of them, Nan F. Nixon, lived in Washington, where Harvard now shared a small office with a group called the Midwestern University Alliance. Nixon's specialties were tax policy and student financial aid, while the rest of Harvard's

Washington corps concentrated on what Shattuck called medical health issues and research integrity issues (a fancy phrase referring to censorship constraints the government proposed to put on researchers funded by the government).

Harvard was actively engaged in lobbying, but Shattuck preferred another term. He called what Nan Nixon and others did "public affairs advocacy. You're never better than the information you produce," he noted. "Here, the capacity to produce is enormous." Several professors in the Economics Department, for example, had helped with the preparation of materials about the impact of tax changes on giving. What was especially important, Shattuck said, was for him "to coordinate the production of information and analysis." He cited the volume of material on tax changes, and said that what Harvard had produced on this had become "the stock information" for others.

"We don't have political action committees, and we won't," he said. "[But] higher education is a great national asset that is delicate and can't be changed. It is a social benefit for everyone." He expected that "the squeeze on higher education we'll feel in the [federal] budget, and tax laws . . . will preoccupy us for the next four to five months, at least." In addition to the Association of American Universities, Harvard was working with the National Association of State Universities and Land Grant Colleges. Harvard's relationship with members of the United States Congress, many of whom had graduated from Harvard, was obviously critical. Shattuck mentioned a program the Kennedy School of Government ran for new members of Congress, who came up to Harvard for a week.

In all, fifty-one members of the ninety-ninth United States Congress were Harvard alumni. Many of that number had graduated from the college, several from the Law School and the Business School, and others claimed a Harvard affiliation through the Kennedy School of Government's Institute of Politics. Senator Moynihan was considered an alumnus because, while a Harvard professor, he had received an honorary M.A.

The list of Harvard members of Congress included eighteen senators.

"On any given day, there are probably two Harvard professors on a plane to Washington," Shattuck said. Recently, he reported, with the emphasis of someone who sees himself near the center of great happenings, the entire staff of the House Science and Technology Committee came to Harvard and the Massachusetts Institute of Technology for two days.

Even the Treasury Department's proposal to eliminate the ceiling on an individual's total charitable gifts would, Harvard calculated, adversely affect donations. Under tax rules in effect at the time, donors' total gift deductions were limited to 50 percent of their adjusted gross income. While this limit would be eliminated under the treasury proposal, so, too, would the present provision that permitted taxpayers to carry over to another year their excess charitable-giving deductions. Thus, Harvard reasoned, the removal of the ceiling — coupled with the elimination of the carryover — would be a disincentive to give among those with high incomes who were making gifts that, under the present system, exceeded the ceiling and were carried over.

Consolidating the various treasury proposals, Harvard showed that, for example, among taxpayers with an adjusted gross income over $200,000, who currently contributed about one-third of all the gifts of assets Harvard received, there would be a 12 percent decrease in such gifts with the elimination of the carryover provision. In general terms, Harvard concluded that "the combined effect of all the provisions would mean a 28 percent decline in the level of cash giving which would otherwise occur, and a nearly 38 percent decline in the giving of appreciated property. The overall decline in charitable contributions by current itemizers would be about 30 percent."

There was a reason for all the numbers, and Harvard understood the reason very well. By late 1984 and early 1985, the desire for some kind of change in the country's income tax system was wide-ranging. Clearly, Harvard felt, there would be a change, in a final form that was not possible to predict. The one way to argue against reforms that, in theory, might seem good for the country was to show, in specific numbers, their effect on one segment of society. But this had to be done without making it seem that only Harvard would be affected. Because the public correctly perceived Harvard as a rich institution, an argument that it alone would be hurt would carry little weight.

No other nonprofit institutions have the human resources to call on that Harvard has. A symphony orchestra, for example, would not have the former chairman of the Council of Economic Advisors on its staff, ready to help with an analysis of the Treasury Department tax changes. And most educational institutions were unlikely to have their own lobbyists in Washington. Typically, such institutions worked in concert, with their interests represented by an umbrella organization such as the Council for Advancement and Support of Education.

Thus, Harvard again was playing a leadership role, but it had to do so very carefully. In his public statements, John Shattuck had to walk a very tight line. It was necessary, on the one hand, to make it clear that this was Harvard talking; it was Harvard that received headlines. However, it was equally necessary to show that not just Harvard's budget was vulnerable here, and it was imperative to skirt around Harvard's abuse of tax-exempt bonds. Harvard never mentioned MATEP in its "public affairs advocacy." Instead, it said that many smaller and less wealthy institutions would be adversely affected by the proposed changes. And so, the argument went, would society, because education, Shattuck stressed, was a social benefit. Harvard just wanted to help others.

Harvard had just taken another "hit," and it was bothering Tom O'Brien. After a long dispute, the university had agreed in December to refund over $4.5 million to the federal government. The amount represented the settlement of "a series of claims and counterclaims" related to the calculation of indirect research costs

— or overhead — in federally sponsored projects at Harvard.

"The dispute," O'Brien said, "involved differences in interpretation of the federal overhead principles and agency regulations relating to technical matters, such as how to calculate depreciation." The settlement had come at a time when Harvard expenditures under federally sponsored projects were continuing to drop on a percentage basis — the figure in 1984 was about 19 percent, down from almost 25 percent in 1980.

The importance of the federal government as a funding source for research at Harvard was difficult to gauge exactly. The amount of money was large — over $110 million in 1984 — but this was apparently not money that Harvard had to have to do business. Rather, the funds supported research that professors needed to do to carry on their work at Harvard. As individuals, they received grants ostensibly based on the intrinsic strengths of their research, but in the aggregate Harvard professors received such funding partly because they taught at Harvard. These funds were thus a kind of huge bonus pool, distributed by the government for its own and society's benefit, and Harvard would invariably do well in getting a large share of the total pool.

"The major source of external support for scientific research at Harvard University," Harvard's 1983–84 *Financial Report* said, "as at essentially all research universities, is the United States government. . . . For the sake of the future of scientific research, the continuation of this partnership is essential.

"Expenditures under federally sponsored projects were $110,196,700 in 1984, representing 18.8% of total University expenditures," the report's section on federally sponsored research continued.

The U.S. Department of Health and Human Services, by far the most significant source of federal research support at Harvard, provided 68.2% of the funds spent on federal projects in 1984. The National Science Foundation provided the second-largest portion of expenditures — 13.2%. . . .

The [financial] report of 1945 . . . indicated that the total operating income of $18,200,000 excluded government contracts of between one and two million dollars. . . .

In his *Report of the President* in 1961, Nathan Pusey noted that Harvard received more income that year from the federal government than from endowment. . . .

In the 1970s, federal support to Harvard for research and development began to decline. . . .

In response to the sudden and tremendous growth of federal support in the 1950s, concerns arose that led to a nationwide study of the effects of federal funds on universities. . . . One of the problems that arose early in the development of federal support for research after World War II was the negotiation of contractual terms and conditions that would be acceptable to both the government and the University. Harvard was sensitive to the potential danger of compromising its academic principles as a result of its increasing involvement with government-sponsored projects. . . . As a result of the growing federal research volume, the University began to articulate principles to guide the conduct of such research. The Faculty of Arts and Sciences has evolved a full set of principles . . . [which] have become the generally accepted standards throughout the University and are applicable to all sponsored projects.

What bothered Tom O'Brien more than the fact of Harvard's research-funding relationship with the government was the increasing amount of paperwork necessary to document the expenditure of such funds. It took time, and it smacked of children's accountability to their parents. Harvard didn't countenance that.

But Harvard also didn't want to lose that portion of federal research money that it took off the top for indirect costs — over $28 million in 1983–84. During the seven-year period from 1974 to 1981, when Harvard received $640 million from the federal government for research, the indirect costs Harvard kept amounted to $160 million. None of that, Harvard stressed, was for salaries. Still, the total was significant; for example, over a third of the cost for building operation and maintenance at Harvard's Medical and Dental schools was funded from this source.

And, coupled with federal funds Harvard received indirectly through financial aid to its students, the government's impact on Harvard's budget was even more significant. Financial aid from all sources to Harvard and Radcliffe undergraduates in 1983–84 was nearly $32 million; in addition, almost $70 million was received by graduate students. Federal student-aid grants, as a percentage of all university student-aid grants, had declined in 1983–84 to about 13 percent for Harvard students and over 9 percent for Radcliffe students, from about 17 percent and over 20 percent, respectively, in 1980–81. But tuition had increased dramatically during that period, so that the total dollar amount of federal financial student aid was higher at the end of the period than at the beginning. John Harvard still did very well by Uncle Sam.

One alternative source of funding research costs at Harvard received widespread publicity after Daniel Steiner issued a memo in 1980 discussing it. The memo addressed the subject of "technology transfer," and the reaction to it, within and without Harvard, was at first quiet, until *The New York Times* ran a story about it. A sharp campus and public debate ensued; eventually, in a dramatic and self-serving about-face, Harvard announced through President Bok that it would not then involve itself in any direct commercial ventures that "transferred technology" to industry — that is to say, enabled Harvard to profit from the work of research scientists by setting up and owning companies that used the applications of that research in, for example, biogenetics. The subject was still alive — it was one of what Steiner called "ongoing policy questions" — but Steiner maintained now that Harvard was "less likely to be affected as significantly as some other institutions. Harvard has relatively little applied science and no engineering department."

No one could say exactly how much money Harvard might have made if, back in 1980, it had licensed a company using the patents of one of Harvard's professors in recombinant DNA. The argument for technology transfer came down to money, just as arguments that technology transfer would help Harvard hold on to and recruit certain research scientists who were being lured by private industry also involved money. But Harvard said it wasn't really worried that its professors were going to leave in droves. What most attracted Harvard to the idea of technology transfer was the possibility it offered Harvard of reasserting its independence from the federal government. A greater fear than dependence on the government, Jim Meketa believed, was the prospect of "honorable gentlemen, underpaid, becoming millionaires" with government Star Wars money.

Paul Martin, who had never left Harvard after his 1948 graduation and who was now dean of the Division of Applied Sciences, spoke with emotion about his calling, which was "something like that of a priest in the church." There was, he continued, "a great satisfaction just from *understanding,* whether or not it will lead to anything." He pointed out that "technology transfer and investing in technology are not the same."

In contrast to the humanities and social sciences, where most of the funds must be provided by Harvard, almost all natural sciences research is funded externally. Harvard has 140 to 150 tenured science professors, and Harvard budgets about $30 million for their research. To fund that would require a lot of unrestricted endowment. The procurement of external research funds was "a major concern," said Martin, since without them a professor can't do research. But "the number of people we hire who don't get some external funding is very small."

Martin spoke by a computer terminal, near a blackboard covered with equations and a bookshelf stocked with titles like *Fluid Dynamics.* "Statistically, Harvard is still doing pretty well. But, again, the fact that a professor has to live with the uncertainty about research funding and promotion to tenure can make it difficult to compete with private industry." Yes, private industry is a "temptation" to some young professors, he said.

The public resolution of the question at Harvard, which Bok wrote about in 1981 in *Harvard Magazine* and, at greater length, in his book *Beyond the Ivory Tower,* left open the possibility of a change in the policy. Bok's chief stated reason for vetoing technology transfer ventures at Harvard was that they could compromise academic standards. "The critical danger is that distinguished investigators will be diverted from their academic work by the prospect of personal gain and will begin to devote themselves to commercial activities in a manner inconsistent with a scholar's proper obligations to the university," he said. It seemed a proper line of reasoning — but how alluring the proposition must initially have been. Harvard had been very tempted by it — the management company had been all set for action — and Daniel Steiner was still asked about it.

"We're both lawyers," Steiner said, speaking of himself and Derek Bok. "We approach problems in a reasonably similar fashion. Certain constitutional values are important to us. I'm not often surprised with his point of view."

Harvard '54, LL.B. '58, Steiner returned to his alma mater in 1969, after practicing law in New York City for five years and serving in Washington for two years with the U.S. Agency for International Development and another two years with the Equal Opportunity Commission. After a year as secretary to the University Committee on Governance, Steiner remained at Harvard at Nathan Pusey's request in the newly created position of general counsel. Over time, supervision of Harvard's personnel, police, and real estate departments were added to Steiner's legal responsibilities, and he gradually added other lawyers to his staff, until, by 1985, there were nine working in a Holyoke Center office. Steiner's title had also been changed to vice president and general counsel.

Steiner is a person of almost invisible presence and undefined power. Known among his colleagues for his wit and sense of humor, Steiner, like Bok, does not often let down his guard. All legal matters, with the exception of those that come up routinely at the Harvard Management Company, go through Steiner, and this in itself is one source of Steiner's authority: he hears more about what is going on at Harvard than do others. Someone whom Bok can trust for advice and information, Steiner also serves as a buffer between Bok and many of his constituencies. When a reporter calls, for example, he can speak for Bok on policy matters such as technology transfer or federal research funding.

"Knowing there will always be critics doesn't mean we don't listen," said Steiner. "But it helps me to get to sleep at night.

"The classic example is South Africa," he continued. "Whatever decision you reach, there are going to be reasonable men and women who will think you're wrong, and may have good reasons for so feeling."

Early on the morning of April 4, 1985, Derek Bok let himself out the locked door of Massachusetts Hall and headed home. Light snow had fallen in Cambridge that week, but the grass in Harvard Yard was green and forsythia was in bloom. The sun shone through scattered clouds, and a chilly breeze blew the bare branches of the trees. It was not long before the Rev. Jesse Jackson would board a plane in Atlanta, bound for Boston. The date was the seventeenth anniversary of the assassination of Martin Luther King Jr., and Jackson was coming to Harvard to protest the university's $565 million investment in companies that do business in South Africa.

By his absence, Bok signified his view that no institutional purpose would be served by his participation in the day's events. He would not be at Logan Airport to greet Jackson, nor would he be present for Jackson's speech. He had other work to do, other concerns. When the afternoon rally began in the yard, and the large crowd chanted, "Derek Bok, get the word, this is not Johannesburg!" he was ensconced in a temporary office on a distant part of the campus. Massachusetts Hall, where four stenciled words in black on the white frame above one of the doors say simply, "Office of the President," would be empty then and under guard.

Now, at 8:15 A.M., while across Harvard Yard the sound of loudspeakers being tested broke the morning stillness, Bok was departing unobtrusively while he could. After the rally, the entrance to the eighteenth-century brick building would be surrounded by protesters, and Bok's presence would be ripe material for the many television news crews covering the occasion. Though the issue of South Africa would not go away, the passion of this particular moment would pass. In the meantime, Bok apparently had more pressing responsibilities to address.

Bok was vilified by some of the people who disagreed with his views. On a previous visit to the university, Jackson had said, "The Harvard–South Africa kinship is a marriage born in hell. The Harvard–South Africa kinship makes crimson turn red; it symbolizes collusion with those who spill the blood of the innocent." To respond in kind might have been tempting, but Bok wasn't one to be drawn into such public debate. He had many worries, but his image as an activist wasn't one of them.

The cafeteria in Dudley House's Lehman Hall was quiet that morning. Harvard students who do not reside at the college are affiliated with Dudley House, which is located in the corner of Harvard Yard adjacent to Harvard Square, across Massachusetts Avenue from the remodeled magazine kiosk, where *Penthouse* is the bestseller. The cafeteria has garish chandeliers, light blue walls, and a great deal of white trim. There is even some white scrollwork. The floor is black linoleum with white specks. The tables are topped with white Formica. The chairs are made of plastic, with shiny steel frames.

Dressed in a white uniform, a man behind the counter made sandwiches to order. He took great care as he placed the ingredients between slices of bread, skewered the sliced halves with toothpicks that had red fringe on one end, and included a pickle when he wrapped each sandwich. He shouted to someone in the nearby kitchen: "Jesse called."

"Who?"

"You know *who*. He's coming to Harvard today. Jesse says he wants a ham and cheese at one-thirty."

Rod MacDougall was still inside Massachusetts Hall as people were gathering by the steps of Memorial Church, across Harvard Yard. Large amplifiers had been set up there, and a banner proclaimed, "Cut Ties With Apartheid Now." Later, MacDougall would be in Boston, across the river in his Harvard Management Company office. "The best thing I can do," he said of the protest, "is clear out of here for twenty-four hours."

The yard was filling up fast. Yellow and green flags. Yellow and red buttons. Professor Adam Ulam, in a heavy overcoat, was walking toward the Faculty Club for lunch. Several professors and their guests were reading magazines and newspapers in the reading room there. It was Maundy Thursday. Jesse Jackson arrived wearing a black trenchcoat. Daniel Steiner, John Shattuck, and David Rosen, the university's public relations director, stood near University Hall, talking among themselves and to others. Rosen was smoking a cigar.

"Harvard shares its honor, credibility, and good name with South Africa," Jackson said. "But Harvard's leadership in disinvestment and divestment can start to weaken South Africa's standing in the world." Crowd estimates varied widely from twenty-eight hundred to eight thousand. Jackson spoke from the steps of Memorial Church, facing Widener Library directly across Tercentenary Theatre (a large, flat quadrangle crisscrossed by paths). The Harvard police chief's car was parked by Sever Hall (designed by Henry Hobson Richardson, newly renovated with campaign funds). There were many other speakers, including one of Robert F. Kennedy's sons. Plainclothes police were numerous. The rally was organized by students, who carried walkie-talkies, looking very filled with a sense of self-importance. Nothing in the rhetoric of the day alluded to any agenda of Jackson's, any hint that he might have been using Harvard as a personal platform as well as a political one.

By the early afternoon, Derek Bok was sequestered at the Kennedy School of Government. It was one of Bok's favorite Harvard places and a kind of symbol of what Harvard in 1985 had become. He was welcome there. If you spent any time at the

Kennedy School, you couldn't help conclude what a safer world this would be if all the world's problems could be analyzed under the purview of one of the school's institutes or programs. Hale Champion, the grand mover for MATEP, had been welcomed back to Harvard there, though his cigar smoke was frowned on by the school's Institute for the Study of Smoking Policy and Behavior, recently funded by a large grant from the Carnegie Foundation.

Bok stubbornly applied his rule of telling the same story to everyone when he wrote or spoke on Harvard's investment in companies that do business in South Africa. Bok had to be consistent. David Rosen gets a phone call from Bok's office whenever something important is going out, such as the announcement of the Baker divestment. Rosen receives an advance copy of such an announcement, to prepare himself for the inevitable press attention.

Bok's tenacity was viewed by some as a testimony to his ability to function under pressure. For all the vitriol of the critics of the South African policy, he had remained calm. There were many reasons that may have kept Bok away from Massachusetts Hall and Harvard Yard on April fourth. He had to worry about how Harvard's fund raising would be affected, how donors and volunteers would feel, many of whom work for companies that do business in South Africa. He had to worry about Harvard's students, many of whose parents hold investments in such companies, whose dividends help pay their children's tuition bills. He had to worry about the university's portfolio and the professionals who manage it. How would their highly sensitive, highly sophisticated work be influenced?

Others viewed Bok's absence differently. "We missed you, Derek," the *Crimson* said the following day. A prisoner of circumstances, perhaps, Bok was also a leader by choice, and he had chosen on April fourth to turn his back on the appearance at Harvard of the most influential black spokesman in the country, who was speaking at Harvard on the gravest human rights question in the world. Bok, who always had the time to make brief remarks upon the dedication of a memorial to a Harvard bene- factor, who had spent countless hours traveling around the coun- try to raise money for the Harvard Campaign, would not face his critics in public. His decision was based on a long-articulated policy that was in turn based, finally, on money. Intellect, not emotion, governed such a policy, but it was intellect of a cool kind, betraying an institutional absence of sensitivity, the fortu- nate looking down upon the unfortunate, the strong patronizing the weak.

Late that night in Harvard Yard, stars were out. A plane flew overhead, soon to land at Logan Airport. The wind blew a scrap of paper across the steps of Widener. It was chilly, but the ground was moist, spring soft. Several hours had passed since Jesse Jackson's voice boomed across this space, his rhetoric slicing the crisp April air, his amplified voice echoing alongside Widener, where a small bridge connects to Houghton Library and its rare books — silence inside there for Keats's manuscripts and Thomas Wolfe's and Ezra Pound's *Cantos* — back all the way to Wigglesworth Hall, a dormitory along Massachusetts Avenue, where the voice was drowned out by the traffic and the MBTA subway. Several hours had passed since that moment. Now, sev- enty-five protesters were camped outside Massachusetts Hall prepared for an all-night vigil. In and around Harvard Square, the Wursthaus, the record shops with Cyndi Lauper and Bruce Springsteen albums in their windows, and the boutiques were closed.

It was quiet by the high concrete columns of Widener: no clash here between words and deeds, Massachusetts Hall and Johan- nesburg, no conflict between money and policy. Inside, tomor- row morning, the day's newspapers would be spindled and hung on racks, later to be classified and filed for easy reference, and elsewhere on the campus Harvard would go about its business.

Happy Birthday, Harvard

DEREK BOK WOULD NOT SCORE highly in an essay contest on the place of the university in American life," retired federal district judge Charles E. Wyzanski Jr. once told me. Tempering a practical admiration for Bok's accomplishments with a sensibility schooled in a lifetime of wide reading and art collecting, the judge continued, "Bok would do much better were the topic the utility of the university."

Nearly eighty years old, Wyzanski is an honorary senior fellow of Harvard and former president of Harvard's Board of Overseers. An elegant, erudite man, who still visits daily his judicial chambers in Boston, Wyzanski is also a neighbor of Bok's, and he spoke about Bok with an opinionated air of fatherly, old-school concern. "I always thought of Bok as a gentleman, as worthy of being president," said Wyzanski. "But anyone who thinks the center of Harvard is the Kennedy School . . ." He shook his head and left the sentence uncompleted, certain his meaning was clear.

Accompanying Bok out of Massachusetts Hall after our last

interview, I walked with him past adjacent Matthews Hall, where someone who seemed not to recognize the president asked for directions to Harvard's Peabody Museum. Very patiently, as though it were a relief to respond to such a request, Bok obliged. Then a professor greeted him and said, pointing to the student with him, who wanted to be introduced to Bok, "He says he's never seen you in Harvard Yard."

Clearly in a hurry now, and annoyed at this trespass, Bok quipped, "That's because I'm always in Miami." Leaving the confused student to puzzle over this bit of humor, Bok exited from the yard, crossed Massachusetts Avenue, and strode to the basement garage in Holyoke Center, where he quickly got into his VW and drove off.

Always on guard, even during a harmless, human encounter, Bok personifies the prideful style of the institution he leads. Especially in its handling of money, Bok's Harvard has to be in control, or appear to others that it is. Whether milking money from its alumni or exploiting opportunities in the investment world, Harvard usually has its own way. Now, with a major milestone in the university's history approaching, Harvard had another chance to make money, and it was capitalizing on this latest fund-raising bonanza.

For several years before 1986, Harvard had been working on plans for its 350th birthday party. Billed as an event of national as well as institutional importance, the occasion was envisioned as a celebration, an opportunity for Harvard to show off in all its finery. But the long prelude to the four-day observance was not without embarrassment for Harvard officials.

In early 1985, when *The New York Times* reported that Ronald Reagan might receive an honorary degree at Harvard's 350th anniversary celebration, the response of many Harvard alumni was immediate. "I'm dismayed," wrote William E. Rowley '37, Ph.D. '68, in a letter to *Harvard Magazine*. "I urge Harvard to call it off." Said another letter writer, Henry A. Francis '60: "If Ronald Reagan speaks at Harvard's 350th or is awarded a Harvard degree, then I shall not be contributing financially to Harvard until my outrage abates."

If the emotional capital of Harvard's alumni is the university's most sensitive resource, it is also the most precious. Recognizing this, the Harvard Corporation settled the Reagan matter by deciding not to give any honorary degrees at all, despite original intentions to award as many as thirty. Other plans for the party proceeded on schedule.

One purpose of the celebration, according to an internal committee memorandum, was "to provide for the happy observance of a significant occasion in the history of Harvard University." Another was "to assess the state of the disciplines at Harvard and in higher education as a whole and to relate their work to the major issues facing our nation and the community of nations in the closing decades of the twentieth century, thereby leaving to posterity an important record of our time."

Once again, Harvard was thinking on the grand scale. Though the celebration was to be "a modest occasion," many speakers were invited, including President Reagan. He declined, but Prince Charles was definitely coming. Symposiums, "making full use of the wisdom that is among us," would form a large part of the program. "A significant number of new publications relating to the history of Harvard" would be issued. But, "it is not enough to commission works of historical scholarship and to publish reports of symposia. Some works of art should remain behind as evidence of the celebration and the university's genuine involvement in the arts." To everything there was one purpose: the glorification of Harvard. It was as though "three hundred and fifty years of higher education in America" were to be reduced to a long weekend, a packaged tour of the academy, and even the painters and poets could come along if they minded their manners.

Lobbying in Washington, Harvard alumni persuaded the United States Postal Service to issue a commemorative stamp. But federal law prohibits such stamps in honor of universities or colleges; the stamp would therefore depict John Harvard. Back in Cambridge, *Harvard Magazine* continued sending out more solicitation flyers to alumni. For a contribution of $25 or more to the magazine, alumni would receive a 350th anniversary coffee mug.

"My place in the world," one alumnus told me, "is still defined by the fact that I went to Harvard. I view Harvard as having provided a social transformation of my life. It affected the way I talk, the stripes on my ties, gave me my closest friends and my wife."

This graduate, intelligent and successful, shared an innocent view of his alma mater with other alumni. And he cared deeply about Harvard. But he was not among those Harvard invited in November 1985 to attend the 350th "gala" ten months later as "official Representatives" of their classes. "While the Celebration is to include all Harvard alumni, faculty, students, staff, and friends from the Boston area," Dean of the Faculty of Arts and Sciences A. Michael Spence wrote in his letter to invitees, "at its core will be a group of Representatives from each of the College classes and graduate schools, distinguished by their service to the University.

"As a Representative, you will have no obligations, only privileges," Spence went on, as though he were a special chum of the surprised recipients, many of whom had no idea why they had been chosen. "I've never been to a reunion, and I don't give much to Harvard," one such alumnus told me. His father, however, was a Harvard administrator.

In an accompanying "fact sheet," class representatives were further defined as people "selected in recognition of their . . . accomplishments in life." Who could disagree with such an unsolicited compliment to himself? It was a perfect come-on, artfully couched in terms to further endear the anointed alumnus to fair Harvard and, of course, to further solidify his status as a member of Harvard's debtor class. The bill would be presented later, when Harvard mounted another fund-raising campaign.

That fall, with the same extravagance being lavished on Harvard's 350th, all alumni began receiving a new publication, *The Harvard College Development Report*. The first issue argued the case for a Harvard College Fund goal of over $17 million. In view of the investment figures for the 1984–85 fiscal year that Harvard was about to announce, this seemed a small sum.

Riding a bull market, Harvard's portfolio that year rose $538 million, or over 23 percent. When this increase was multiplied through the continued strong market in late 1985 and early 1986, Harvard's endowment had about doubled since the decade began. Since during that time Harvard had successfully conducted a campaign to raise $350 million, one Harvard watcher concluded that Harvard could in effect lay claim to having mounted a $700 million campaign.

The *Financial Report to the Board of Overseers of Harvard College* in which the 1984–85 figures were summarized noted the recent formation of a Debt Management Committee and included a lengthy, self-serving explanation of Harvard's use of tax-exempt debt, with scant acknowledgment of the impact of MATEP. "These borrowings," the report said of the MATEP bonds, "financed the plant at the lowest possible interest cost and restored the General Operating Account's liquidity, which had been reduced by its internal advances for the plant's construction." No mention was made of Harvard's latest debt issue — for $140 million — since it had been placed after the 1984–85 fiscal year. That borrowing brought Harvard's total debt to $780 million, at a time when the United States Congress was considering a proposal to cap an institution's tax-exempt debt at $150 million.

Harvard gave no public thanks for this early birthday present from the United States tax system that made such debt profitable, nor did the university allude to this further position of financial strength in its promotion of the anniversary fete. Instead, in such announcements as the "350th News and Notes" in *The Harvard University Gazette,* Harvard reported that, "Tommy Walker, noted for his pyrotechnic and special effects wizardry during the opening and closing ceremonies of the 1984 Olympic Games in Los Angeles, will produce and direct the 350th Celebration 'spectacular' in Harvard Stadium. The event, on Saturday night, September 6, will combine music, pageantry, multi-media projections, and laser and fireworks displays. John Williams and the Boston Pops Orchestra will be joined by other musicians and performers, including Harvard's performing groups." Harvard again was selective in what it said about itself, despite the seal of Veritas, or truth, that graced the portals of its gates and the headings of its publications.

"As a symbol of his belief in the true function of a university," wrote Samuel Eliot Morison in his *Three Centuries of Harvard,* "President [Josiah] Quincy was delighted when beginning research for the great History of Harvard University to find in the archives the first rough sketch for a College Arms, VERITAS on three books. The announcement was made at the bicentennial celebration [in 1836]; and in 1843, an ugly version of the design was formally adopted by the Corporation as their seal." Quincy's successor, Edward Everett, "conceived an intense dislike of everything that his predecessor had done," and the seal was banished. "It slept again until 1885," said Morison, "when, largely as the result of two vigorous sonnets by Dr. [Oliver Wendell] Holmes read before the Harvard Club of New York, *Veritas* was brought forth once more." Now, incorporating the numerals 350 within that seal, Harvard's logo for its 350th anniversary conspicuously placed the university's motto before a world that was asked to applaud what Hooks Burr, chairman of the 350th Anniversary Commission and chief marshal of the 350th Celebration, called "a landmark in this country's history of education."

With tuition increases finally slowing down, a program of deferred maintenance well under way, a lock on the tax-exempt bond market secured, a major fund-raising campaign completed, and a booming endowment growing apace, Harvard at 350 was in excellent financial health. The ratio of its endowment — or the "equity base," as George Siguler liked to call it — to the annual budget was now about 5 to 1, and this landmark figure was getting better. Siguler, who had calculated that his own "share" of that equity, in the form of his pension, was about 1/10,000th, argued that "the financial character of the place has changed. Harvard in 1986 is at its wealthiest." Though in what form, and with what spirit, it was impossible to predict, the university would be around for many more years to come. Making money, Harvard was giving new meaning to an old term: what one Harvard official had called with nostalgia, "the golden age of academia," had been reborn.

Acknowledgments

Though relatively little of the great wealth of Harvard literature, past and present, is specifically about the subject of this book, it was a help to me in my research. Most of the sources I used I have cited in the text, but I wish also to acknowledge E. J. Kahn's *Harvard: Through Change and Through Storm* (1969) and David Owen's "State-of-the-Art Panhandling" (*Harper's,* August 1982). *The Harvard Crimson,* especially the reporting of Peter J. Howe and Joseph Kahn, *Harvard Magazine,* and a number of Harvard's own publications, including *The Harvard Book* (1982), *The Harvard University Gazette,* and several volumes of the *Financial Report to the Board of Overseers of Harvard College,* were invaluable. Seymour Harris's *The Economics of Harvard* (1970) and Samuel Eliot Morison's *Three Centuries of Harvard* (1936) were trusted companions.

My debts to people are many and deep. A few of the people I interviewed, many of them several times, spoke with me on the condition that their names would not appear in the book. My thanks to those among them who took a special interest in what

I was doing must, therefore, go unacknowledged here. All the names that do appear are real, of course, and my narrative of events, except where I have acknowledged other sources, is based on my own interviews and observations. Two people, Harvard classmates James Meketa and Stuart Schoffman, I must single out for their counsel and encouragement, and a third, George Putnam, for his hospitality and tireless response to my requests.

For their time, I thank William Alfred, David Aloian, Henry J. Ameral, Donald D. Beane, John T. Bethell, Derek Bok, Michael T. Boland, Francis H. Burr, Walter M. Cabot, Hale Champion, John R. Chase, Robert Coles, David Dearborn, Donald Fleming, Fred L. Glimp, Norton and Rikki Grubb, Andrew Heiskell, Deane W. Lord, Roderick M. MacDougall, Blue Magruder, Paul C. Martin, Thomas O'Brien, Nils P. Peterson, Nathan M. Pusey, Thomas M. Reardon, Henry Rosovsky, John Shattuck, Robert Shenton, George W. Siguler, Ira Silverman, A. Michael Spence, Daniel Steiner, Robert G. Stone Jr., Bing Sung, Michael G. Thonis, Bruce Wilcox, and Charles E. Wyzanski Jr. None of these people gave their sanction to what I wrote, and some of them will disagree with the conclusions I have drawn, but I am grateful to all of them.

I also wish to thank Austin Olney, Helena Bentz, Nancy Boardman, Craig Bonner, Elaine Breor, Laurence Cooper, Deborah J. Earle, Barbara B. Ford, William N. Fuller, Kenneth Hale-Wehmann, William E. Hart, Peter D. Ickes, David Irons, Elizabeth Keul, Robert Manning, the late Frederic F. Milne, Tami Nason, James Petrin, Peg Pontes, Roberta Pryor, Barbara Putnam, Harriet C. Rogers, David Rosenbaum, Jody Ryan, Thomas Scanlon, R. Marshall Schell, Jackie Scott, Evelyn Smith, Ed Socha, Ann Stewart, Beverly Sullivan, the late John William Ward, John A. Ware, Douglas C. Wilson, Betty Woodward, Meg Worcester, Sarah Wright, and the librarians of Hampshire College, the Harvard University Archives, and the Robert Frost Library at Amherst College. I apologize to anyone whose name I have inadvertently left out.

My family, including my mother, Ruth, my sister, Astrid, my brother, Nils, and my sister-in-law, Madeline, gave me their love and support when I needed it most. My son, Christian, and daughter, Anna, reminded me there are more important things in the world than writing a book.

Two people sustained me from beginning to end, and their names appear at the front of this book. While neither is responsible for any mistakes I may have made, both contributed immeasurably to my writing. No writer could be more fortunate than to have as his editor Richard Todd, whose patience, advice, tact, and friendship saw me through countless critical moments. He believed in this book when it was just an idea and nurtured it during a long and sometimes arduous birth. My wife, Bonnie, gracefully and selflessly bore the brunt of my most difficult days and nights. She was a careful and demanding reader, a constant center of good sense and abundant cheer. I owe her more thanks than, with my love, I can give.